Catherine

THE NOEL STREATFEILD SUMMER HOLIDAY BOOK

For other titles in the Target Series see end pages

THE NOEL STREATFEILD SUMMER HOLIDAY BOOK

A collection of stories and poems to while away the long, hot summer days . . .

Illustrated by Sara Silcock

a division of
Universal-Tandem Publishing Co., Ltd.,
14 Gloucester Road, London SW7 4RD

First published in Great Britain by J. M. Dent & Sons, Ltd., 1973

First published in this edition by Universal-Tandem Publishing Co., Ltd., 1975

ISBN 0 426 10524 9

Printed in Great Britain by The Anchor Press Ltd., and bound by Wm. Brendon & Son Ltd., both of Tiptree, Essex

Contents

NOEL STREATFEILD

My Summer Holidays

Just saying the words 'summer holiday' gives the sort of feeling I imagine a bud has when it thinks, 'Soon I shall burst open. Soon I shall be a flower.'

I have had this feeling about summer holidays all my life, which is odd for we had many disastrous holidays when I was a child.

We all went away for the month of August. When I say all I mean all. We four children, our father and mother, our dog Spot and the 'staff'. In those days, however poor you were, people like parsons, which was what my father was, always had 'staff'. Somebody to look after us children—a nurse when we were small and later on a governess—and someone to cook and another to do the housework.

I think the weather must have changed since those days. Now it is possible to have glorious weather in Britain in August. People go and live in caravans or holiday camps or go trekking or riding and come back positively blistered by the sun. Yet when I was a child I only remember one hot August; during all the others it rained and rained and rained. It is bad enough when you spend a rainy holiday at home, but in a not very nice country or seaside house, with very few books in it—none of which you want to read, and only one table so you can't lay out a farm or jigsaw puzzle—life can be very trying, and our holidays were mostly that.

Today of course many of you do not know what Britain is like in August. You fly off to exotic places with strange-sounding names. You may be reading this on a sun-soaked beach or on an oasis in the middle of a desert, on top of a mountain or in a boat. The world is almost anybody's oyster, and quite often it is cheaper to fly to Spain or some other warm spot than it is to go to a holiday resort at home.

Mind you, it would not be fair to deny we did go to some heavenly places. I remember a cottage in Devonshire. The cottage itself was horrible—no running water, no bathroom, and the lavatory outside so we were scared to visit it after dark. We did have baths because we had brought a bath with us, but mostly for washing we depended on the sea, in which we were forced to swim every day no matter how cold the water.

It is that walk to the sea that has stayed with me always. It was a twisting, turning path with first earth and moss under foot and then, as we came nearer the sea, silvery sand. Never in my life have I known such a variety of flowers nor such wild strawberries as grew in that lane. The strawberries were almost as large as the garden type and tasted delicious.

Then there was a holiday in Wales. It may have been a beautiful place but our cottage was desperately uncomfortable—even worse than the one in Devon for the lavatories for the whole village street were outside, set side by side and, as they were unnumbered and exactly alike, it was terribly easy to step into the wrong one to be met by a shower of abuse in Welsh.

I particularly remember Sundays in that village. We were of course taken to church properly dressed but with beach clothes left with our bathing things in the porch. In that church we had two sermons. The first very short in almost basic English (that was for the visitors), the second enormously long in Welsh. If you have ever sat through a long service where you were preached to in a language you did not understand you will know just how we felt; and for those Welsh sermons we had to be especially well behaved for my father thought a swinging leg or fidgeting might be interpreted as rudeness on the part of the English.

Sunday evenings in that village made up for Welsh sermons. Then all the locals and many others from miles around went down to the beach to sing. We and other visitors sat on a cliff top to listen. Even now, if I stretch my ears, I can hear those Welsh hymns carried back over the years: the glorious Welsh voices accompanied by the slip-slap of the waves and the mewing of seagulls. I can travel all over the world but I will not match the beauty that I remember of those Sunday evenings.

Our two worst holidays were in Derbyshire and in Cambridgeshire. Even now I have never persuaded myself to revisit Derbyshire. I know it is beautiful and much of it historically interesting but my memories hold me back. We stayed in a horrible little red brick house on the side of a wind-swept hill. There seemed nowhere to dry anything though we children were always soaked, for not only did it rain all the time but we played all day in the only local place of interest—a pond. This pond was exactly opposite our house and had sunk in it a large red canister in which we decided there was buried treasure. Almost the last day of our stay we managed to land that canister and there was nothing in it at all except mud. It was the final blow and from then onwards poor Derbyshire became to us 'that awful Derbyshire' or 'it was as terrible as Derbyshire.'

Cambridgeshire was a bad holiday because of the weather. Not for once because it was wet but because it was so blazingly hot. Cambridgeshire is a very flat county and my father had decided it would be the perfect place to bicycle. So with bicycles added to our luggage, to Cambridgeshire we all went. The heat wave went on day after day with temperatures up in the 80s and 90s. Wherever our water supply came from it dried up and so, I am afraid, did our tempers. The shops were far away and when someone had sweated their way to them nobody had the appetite to eat what was served. Worst of all we were made to wear too many clothes. Today as you sunbathe wearing almost nothing, it is impossible for you to imagine what clothes used to be like. First on the list was decency. Children must be properly covered. Oh dear, those vests and liberty bodices, knicker linings and knickers and, after we reached double figures, woollen stockings! Other years we had not minded because it was usually wet and nearly always cold, but that Cambridgeshire year how we suffered.

Father was working on us at that time to take an interest in brass rubbings. Now brass rubbing has become almost a business, especially amongst our visitors from abroad, so there are special shops which sell all that brass rubbers need. When I was a child brass rubbing was a hobby and all you needed was to find a brass memorial set in a church floor. This you covered with a large sheet of wall-lining paper, then you rubbed it evenly all over with a lump of cobbler's wax. I don't think cobblers sell wax now. It really is a fascinating occupation for it is like watching magic to see the brass memorial appear on your sheet of paper. It is so fascinating that today brass rubbing has become immensely popular as well as a money maker, so there are no well-known brasses which you can rub without permission—usually in writing.

Personally that year in Cambridgeshire I was nearly put off brass rubbing for life for it really was too hot for bicycling and all I wanted to do when we arrived at the church where the brass belonged—which was usually miles away—was to lie down in the shade under a tree.

As a climax to that holiday my brother picked up some fearsome germ which meant he was not just seen by the local doctor but the medical officer of health arrived. All the drinking water was tested and as quickly and quietly as possible we were hurried back home in quarantine. What only we children knew was that whatever my brother caught our dog Spot had it too. Of course he knew nothing about quarantine so he must have infected other dogs for miles around.

That is enough about my summer holidays so now let's have a story. I have chosen a really summer holiday one to start with. It is written by Ursula Moray Williams. Ursula Moray Williams is a lovely writer, a writer who never quite keeps both feet on the ground. Other writers keep explaining how things happen, but not Ursula Moray Williams. She knows they happened as she knows you know they happened and who else is there to worry about?

One of the qualities that make a good writer is the care with which, often in quite few words, they build relationships between people. As you read this story notice the affection that grows between Robert and Mrs Williams. Notice even more carefully the complete and immediate understanding there is between Grandmère and Robert, and all done so simply you know it must have really happened. When I received this story from Ursula Moray Williams I was enchanted, for I was sure you would love it as much as I do.

URSULA MORAY WILLIAMS

The Outlaws

The French schools began their holidays early in July.

Robert, on an exchange summer holiday to the Williams family, had to content himself for nearly two weeks with very little company of his own age until David Williams should come home from boarding-school.

Jenny and Sarah Williams were at day school from half-past nine until teatime. It was the only peace that Robert had. When they were at home they dragged him round the stables, hoisted him onto their ponies and made fun of his accent.

'Rob-bair!' they repeated when he pronounced his name. In England they called it Robbut. And not content with saying *his* name wrong they criticized him when he mispronounced theirs.

'Jenni! Sairah!' he could manage, but his tongue betrayed him when he tried to say 'Williams'. 'Vill-ee-ams,!' Robert said, but the girls insisted he should pronounce it Willyums. Robert wished he had a surname five syllables long to confound the mocking English accents. Nobody had much difficulty in pronouncing Legros.

The girls were older than he. They were kind in a boisterous and patronizing way, but they beat him at everything they did together: at tennis, at swimming—even at clock golf.

When they were absent Robert followed Mrs Williams comfortably round the house, went shopping with her, took the dog out and watched television. She reminded him of his mother and he was very nearly perfectly happy. But Mrs Williams was under the constant misapprehension that he must be bored in her company. 'Only another week till David comes!' she would tell him as if they were making a tremendous joint effort to keep their chins up until David arrived, and every half hour during the afternoon she looked at the clock and said encouragingly: 'The girls will soon be home!'

The girls put such energy into everything they did that Robert felt sure his father would have approved of them. It was Monsieur Legros who had pounced upon the sentence in Mrs Williams's letter offering tennis and riding at their home. 'Le sport', his father called it rather reverently. He approved of 'le sport'.

In return the Legros offered sailing and 'le water ski' at their summer house to David when he should come back to France with Robert in the middle of August. Robert hated both, but since arriving at the Williamses he had decided that either was preferable to riding.

Jenny and Sarah put him onto a pony called 'Greenfly' and took him into a paddock where the grass was soft. They put a hard hat on his head that belonged to David, but David had quite a different kind of head. The hat slipped forward onto Robert's nose or shot off backwards and got left behind.

The girls made a little jump from brushwood, and encouraged Greenfly to jump over it. Robert fell off and they put him back in the saddle because they said it was bad for him not to mount again immediately after a fall. It seemed to Robert the best of all possible reasons for staying on the ground, but even after he took a second tumble they persuaded him to get on again. When he fell off a third time they said it was bad for the horse, and let him retire to the railings and watch. Both girls rode very well, and by the trophies hanging round the stables and in the house Robert had a strong suspicion that David did too.

Robert wished now that he had made himself proficient at sailing and water ski-ing last summer when he had had the chance, so that he would have something to excel at when David came back to France with him. For nobody could possibly be so bad at either sport as he was. David was exactly his own age, but his family, his enthusiasm and his British education had almost certainly given him an advantage over Robert when it came to 'le sport'. He almost dreaded David coming to his home.

The girls had joined in the chorus now. 'David will be here on Friday!' they chanted on Monday morning. There was a note of relief in their voices that Robert did not miss, for he knew they were getting tired of having him at their heels. They only offered him one set of tennis now, after tea, and then made excuses or played singles with each other.

On Tuesday morning came a letter from David's school that caused consternation around the breakfast table.

'David,' the school matron wrote, 'has had measles, but not very badly. If you can fetch him by car the doctor says he can travel on Wednesday and the journey won't hurt him.'

David's parents looked so concerned that Robert became anxious.

'David . . . is he *malade*?' he inquired.

'He has *spots*!' Jenny said in the loud clear voice she reserved for explaining things to Robert. She dabbed at her face with her finger. 'Have you had spots?'

Robert shook his head. Childish diseases had passed him by.

'Worse and worse!' said Sarah. She exchanged a look with her sister that Robert might not have noticed if Mrs Williams had not said '*Sarah!*' so reprovingly that he knew Jenny must be getting at him again.

'David won't be able to do anything with Robert, because of giving him measles!' said Sarah, as if her mother had not spoken. 'And David won't be able to do anything at all. He'll miss the cricket match on the twenty-ninth and the garden fête and gymkhana this Saturday. I suppose Jen and I can go to the Pony Club camp as we've both had measles, but you do realize, Mummy, that if Robert gets measles from David he'll be here for most of the holidays?'

'And David won't be able to go back with him to France!' added Jenny.

'Well, never mind about that,' said Mrs Williams, looking embarrassed and pushing the breakfast things about. Jenny and Sarah always behaved as if Robert understood no conversation that was not directed at him loudly and personally. Mrs Williams took the opposite view, that he understood everything, and nothing must be said that could possibly hurt his feelings as a foreigner and a visitor. The truth lay somewhere in between. Robert perfectly understood the situation that had arisen, and was trying to remember the number of days that had separated him from his cousins having measles during the previous summer holidays. He also understood without being told that Jenny and Sarah did not want his visit prolonged by one day if they had to undertake the hospitality. He heartily agreed with them.

'I know!' said Sarah. 'He can go to Grandmère till David is better!'

'Great!' said Jenny. 'He'd enjoy that.'

'I think that is a very good idea!' said Mrs Williams. 'He would have a lovely time with Grandmère!'

'Let's ring her!' Sarah said, 'Shall I do it?'

'*I* will!' said Mrs Williams.

'Who will ring what?' said Mr Williams who had been reading his papers. He was a solicitor, and he hardly ever spoke to Robert, but when he did he was always kind and polite.

'We don't want Robert to be in quarantine and get measles from David!' Mrs Williams said. 'So it might be a good idea for him to go and stay with Grandmère for a few days until David gets over it.'

'And would Robert like that?' Mr Williams said, pronouncing his name in the French way and looking straight at him.

'I think I go home to France!' said Robert decidedly.

'Well now you know what Robert would like!' said Mr Williams, picking up his papers. 'Come on, girls, I'm leaving the house in three minutes and I shan't wait.'

Jenny and Sarah dashed after him, squealing.

'My mother has a very nice home,' Mrs Williams said across

the empty breakfast table. 'We call her Grandmère because she loves France so much, but her real name is Lady Swayne. She will love to have you. If you stayed with her just till David isn't infectious any more you can come back here afterwards and go off to France together just as was planned. Don't you think that would really be quite a good idea?'

'Yes, madame!' said Robert, subdued.

'I'll go and telephone Grandmère and see if she can have you from tomorrow, when we fetch David!' Mrs Williams said. 'It would all fit in so well if she could.'

'Yes, madame,' said Robert. He began to clear away the breakfast things. Mrs Williams came back very quickly from the telephone.

'No reply!' she said. 'Grandmère often goes shopping on a Tuesday. I'll ring again directly after lunch.'

During the morning Mrs Williams and Robert made fifteen pounds of raspberry jam. Robert wrote the labels and sealed the tops. During the whole operation, while Mrs Williams chatted, he was thinking hard. He forgave Mrs Williams for having a situation forced upon her that was not of her making, but he strongly resented being discussed at the breakfast table like a superfluous object, and disposed of as if he had been a parcel to be sent here and there. He felt that his parents ought to have been brought into the discussion. They might not approve of his being sent away into the house of a French-speaking old lady they had never met. They had been particularly anxious that he should not speak any French at all while he was in England. He tried to explain this to Mrs Williams, but it was really too difficult, and too much trouble to fetch a dictionary with his fingers covered with raspberry jam. He slaughtered thirteen wasps and earned Mrs Williams's grateful thanks, for she was frightened of them.

When he had disposed of the wasps he went upstairs and packed his suitcase. He discovered that for the first time since he left Paris he was feeling homesick. He had felt strange, of course, for the first few days, and chilled by Jenny and Sarah's mockery, but they had been kind after their own fashion, and Mrs Williams had been affectionate and very kind indeed. Slowly he had settled in, and now he was to be uprooted and transplanted. He was not even to be allowed to meet David.

And his parents knew nothing about it! He had no doubt that Mrs Williams would telephone his mother when all was settled, but meanwhile he felt as if he had been dropped into a void, as if he belonged to nowhere and nobody. Tears smarted at the back of his eyes accompanied by a band of grief that constricted his throat and broke into a sob that he tried to stifle by burrowing inside his suitcase.

His fingers closed on the familiar shape of his return air ticket. At once his desolation seeped away. He felt like a prisoner who has accidentally discovered the key of his cell.

The Williams family had met him at the airport, only seven miles from their home. In Mr Williams's fast car it had seemed even less. All he had to do was walk to the airport, change his ticket for the evening flight and telephone his father when he arrived. He would then explain to his family that David had measles and he could not stay any longer. They would much rather have him at home he felt sure. Or nearly sure. David could come over later. Madame Legros was not likely to object to that just because Robert had returned a few days early. He packed very rapidly and completely.

For lunch, Mrs Williams cooked him the English sausages that he liked so much, and he realized that he loved her dearly. When she spoke of the things they would do when David had finished having measles and Robert came back again he agreed with her whole-heartedly rather than face the pain of knowing that this was their last meal together.

'Such a hot afternoon!' she said as they cleared the table and washed up. 'I'm afraid we shall have a storm before dark. Are you going to sunbathe? Only two hours and the girls will be back!'

She went away to telephone 'la Grandmère'. Robert went to his bedroom, picked up his suitcase and left the house by the back stairs to catch the five o'clock plane from Hardington to Paris that was charted on his ticket. He wrote 'Thank you very much!' on a piece of paper and left it under his pillow.

It was a hot and sultry afternoon. Since one o'clock the sun had slowly eased itself behind a blanket of haze. Robert hurried through the orchard where caterpillars, suspended on long threads, brushed his face before dropping limply to the ground, all their labours shattered. He skirted the meadow where the girls had made their practice jumps, glad that no ponies came galloping to greet him. They were grazing elsewhere.

The suitcase was heavy, as suitcases invariably are, but Robert disregarded this. He changed it from hand to hand as he strode along, finding it less unbearable than the folded mackintosh clinging with disagreeable moisture to his neck and shoulders already clammy with heat.

The girls had taken him, jogging uncomfortably on a pony, through woods that later joined the Hardington road. From the far side they had pointed out the airfield on the distant horizon, and Robert took this way now, thankful for the shade of the trees and absence of traffic that had passed him on the main road without ceasing. Nobody took the slightest notice of the hesitating hand he raised to beseech a lift. Perhaps people did not hitchhike in England, Robert wondered.

The great woods! The beeches and the oaks! reminding him vaguely of the forests south of Paris, at Barbizon. Trees, he thought, were like kind quiet ladies, like Mrs Williams who was good to him, while the prickly spiky bushes were like Jenny and Sarah. He turned in sudden panic, half expecting to see or hear them galloping up the track on their ponies, but Jenny and Sarah were ending their summer term at school and the woods were empty, except for buzzing insects and a sudden green woodpecker, calling for rain.

He heard the first roll of thunder as a warm raindrop fell on his forehead, and stopped, prudently, to put on his mackintosh. The sky above the trees was very black. Would the plane leave for Paris if there were a thunderstorm? He did not want to hang about the airport waiting. It would be natural for the Williams family to make inquiries when they found him gone, and it would be humiliating to say the least if he were found and apprehended in public. Nothing, he told himself, would now prevent him from boarding the plane, but let it be with dignity and a minimum of fuss.

Sheet lightning lit up the woods. Storms could be unpleasant but Robert had had his baptism of them while climbing in the high mountains with his uncle, a sport that he enjoyed with all his heart and soul. After the fury of the Alps he had little dread of a small British thunderstorm. It was however inconvenient as the rain gathered force and began to seep down the back of his neck. It poured off his suitcase into his shoes. The ends of his trousers were sopping wet. His smart new mackintosh, called showerproof, was not standing up to the deluge that now fell out of the sky, and as the trees were sparse at that point Robert left the track to find shelter where they grew more thickly. Then he smelt woodsmoke.

It was a sweet and comfortable smell. Robert thought in terms of a charcoal burner's hut where he could shelter, but at least he hoped to find a British workman with some kind of roof over his head.

Not quite so solid, but in its way quite as satisfactory was the sight he saw when he thrust his way through the bushes and found a small car.

The car itself was familiar, being a continental model that he saw constantly in and about Paris. Beside it was pitched a small tent. From a nearby tree projected a canvas roof, too restricted to protect the fire underneath it that an elderly lady was energetically trying to keep alive.

She lay almost flat on the ground, blowing so hard at the fire that her eyes were closed and her face bright pink. She must, Robert thought, be a tinker woman, until something about her clothes and the atmosphere of the tiny encampment told him that this was no tinker, but an English 'madame' very busy 'making le camping'.

The fire smouldered, sulked and hissed. The lady blew and hissed back. The rain poured down and she took not the slightest notice of Robert. He longed for the shelter of the tent or of the car, if it were only for five minutes or until the rain stopped, but he did not like to introduce himself.

Finally he remembered passing some bundles of birch cuttings only a short way behind him, and birch wood burned well, as he knew from camping with his uncle. He turned back, and presently stood at the lady's side holding an armful of birch twigs almost dry under his mackintosh. He had prudently left his suitcase sheltering underneath her car.

The lady had paused to wipe her streaming eyes. She stared at him in astonishment.

'Permettez!' Robert said gently, and lowered himself to the ground. He pushed the birch twigs underneath the grumbling wood ends and slowly they began to burn. More twigs, more wood, the sullen little fire sprang into life, and as it burned the old lady hurled a small kettle on top of it with a glee that was almost vindictive.

'Wonderful!' she exclaimed. 'We'll have a cup of tea! Come and keep dry inside the car!'

They rushed for shelter. Robert felt every seam now in his sodden clothing, every inch of his squelching socks. He grabbed his suitcase and dragged it into the car behind him.

'And who may you be?' the lady asked him.

'Please?'

'What is your name?'

Too close, too close to the Williamses to tell his real name, thought Robert. What if the lady was a personal friend who had heard all about him?

'André,' he said. 'André Prevost.'

'Oh!' she said, staring at him. 'You are a French boy?'

'*Oui madame!*' he answered automatically.

'And where are you going?' she asked, looking at the suitcase.

'I go to the airport!' said Robert readily. 'I catch the flight to Paris. Five o'clock,' he added to show her that he had himself completely organized.

'Not on a *Tuesday*!' the lady exclaimed. 'Mondays, Wednesdays and Fridays, but there is no flight to Paris from Hardington on a Tuesday.'

Inside him Robert's heart took a rush downwards to his shoes. Such a thought had never crossed his mind.

'The kettle's boiling!' shrieked the lady. She bolted into the rain, fetched a teapot from the tent, and returned to the car with two mugs, a milk bottle and the steaming brew. 'One moment!' she cried, and bolted back for the sugar.

The tea was almost as welcome as coffee. Robert clasped his damp fingers round the mug and tried to pretend he was not feeling desperate. The lady drank and said nothing. Outside, the rain poured down, but rather more gently now.

'Thank you, madame!' Robert said, preparing to go. Then he remembered he had nowhere to go to.

'Where are you off to?' she asked. 'Back where you came from?'

He shook his head automatically. Anything but that. Such ignominy! Such humiliation! He could almost hear the muffled laughter of Jenny and Sarah behind his back. Though his chin remained rigid tears pricked behind his eys.

'Are you fond of camping?' the lady asked. He nodded violently.

'Then perhaps you would like to camp here with me until your plane goes tomorrow afternoon?' she said politely.

Above, the sky was inky black and solid, but Robert could have sworn that the sun came out at that moment.

'*Oui madame . . . s'il vous plaît!*' he murmured, as the awful gulf beneath his feet closed, leaving him once more on solid ground.

'You will have to sleep in the car!' she told him, 'and I shall have to get some more food from the village. Will you come with me?'

He hesitated. Twenty-four hours to go, and in any one of them he might be discovered. Better remain hidden deep in the woods.

'I stay here, madame!' he said. 'I make a good fire and . . . and . . .' he indicated the amount of wood that he meant to collect in her absence. The little car bubbled into life and rattled away out of sight.

When the lady returned, carrying a string bag full of groceries, the sun was shining again, turning the wet tree trunks into pillars of gold. The wood looked like a cathedral. Robert had peeled potatoes and changed into dry clothes from his suitcase. His hostess was delighted with him.

'I have sausages!' she told him. 'And peaches and cornflakes and chocolate biscuits and coffee! And Mars bars to eat in bed. Do you like Mars bars?'

The Williamses had not introduced Robert to Mars bars but he said: 'Yes, madame!' with enthusiasm.

'There's only one thing,' the lady said. 'I haven't really got enough blankets for us both. I shall have to go back to my house and get some.'

He stared, not having connected her with a home of her own, but blankets were not so important as supper, and he had just built a splendid fire. As they ate, although she asked no questions, he told her a little bit about his holiday, with friends ... far from here, he explained, half in French and half in English ... but there was illness in the family and it was necessary for him to go home early.

'I see,' she said with feeling. 'What a shame!'

Dusk was falling as they washed up the supper plates in a stream muddied by the rain. 'Don't drink that!' she said. 'You can have some wine. I expect you often drink it in France.'

The wine made him so sleepy he would have liked to go to bed, but the dark wet woods seemed so lonely that he chose instead to go with her in her little car to fetch the blankets. They took a track he did not recognize and drove a long way among the trees without meeting any other traffic. Then they travelled a short distance down a main road till they came to a drive gate. The drive wound up a sloping hill to a very beautiful old house. The lady drove round to the back and produced a large key.

'Is this your house?' Robert asked, astonished.

'Yes. There is nobody here. Come in!'

They entered the house by the back door, almost tiptoeing in, Robert thought. It was not yet dark, but deep twilight. The lady switched on no lights as they crossed a hall into a large sitting-room, with comfortable sofa and chairs, beautiful furniture, old pictures and a grand piano.

While the lady plucked cushions and travelling rugs from the sofa and chairs Robert stood peering round the room in the dusk. The first thing he recognized was a large photograph of Jenny and Sarah on their ponies, standing on top of the grand piano. He jumped quite violently at the sight of them. The lady turned round.

'You know . . . these people?' Robert quavered.

'Those are my grandchildren,' the lady said calmly. 'But it is quite all right, Robert, there is nothing to worry about. When I was in the village I telephoned to my daughter and told her you were with me and we were going away for a little holiday together. She thinks we are on tour.' As Robert still stared she added in French: 'I knew you were staying there, my dear, and your initials were on your suitcase. It wasn't difficult to guess who you were. But we all have our independent ideas, you know. *I* like to get away from friends and relations now and again and live my own life exactly as I please. I adore camping!'

'And I do!' said Robert fervently.

'Good. So we will camp. And nobody shall call us silly old lady and silly young boy. We will do as we like. *Bon?*'

'*Très bon!*' said Robert, delighted.

'It has worked out very well!' the Grandmère said. 'They wanted to send you to me and now you have come! And we will let them think that we have gone away so we shall not have lots of horses galloping through our camp every morning . . . eh?' They laughed together. 'And if you want to catch the plane to Paris tomorrow, or on Friday, or the next Monday, it is all the same to me,' the Grandmère concluded. '*Bon?*'

'*Très bon!*' said Robert, entirely happy.

They lived like outlaws until the end of the week. At night they crept back to the house to raid the larder and the frozen cabinet in case anyone mentioned their shopping at the village store. On the Wednesday afternoon when the Grandmère asked if he wanted to catch the Paris plane Robert was quite startled.

'No, thank you, madame, I will go on Friday,' he told her.

They prattled together in French, and to compensate she brought English story books from the house, which they read together in the evenings. She gave him English lessons which Mrs Williams had never had time for, although she had always meant to do so.

The Grandmère taught him more about camping and the woods than he had ever dreamed of, and took him early in the morning and in the dusk of the evening to fly fish on a small stream behind the woods. During the day he practised the intricate art of casting with a fly rod, using a feather tied to the end of the line that he learned to drop lightly here and there, now on a daisy, now on a wild strawberry plant. The little trout they caught were grilled on the fires Robert made so successfully. They tasted better than anything he had eaten in Paris.

One day when they were gathering toadstools to eat (the Williamses called them all poisonous, but Robert and the Grandmère knew which were the edible kinds) they heard horses' hooves, and flung themselves flat in the bushes just in time, as Jenny and Sarah galloped by. Afterwards they could

hardly stop laughing as they crept back to their camp by a roundabout route in case the girls came back again.

The Grandmère brought a folding bed from the house and Robert slept in the open. Never would he forget the dawn choruses . . . or the soft darkness that spread itself across his blankets while owls called and recalled each other, and mosquitoes hummed away in discontent, repulsed by the oil of lavender with which the Grandmère drenched his pillow. And just now and then he was awakened by soft rain damping his brow that sent him scampering for the car with his blankets clutched underneath his chin.

'Shall you catch the plane tomorrow?' the Grandmère asked him on Thursday.

'*Non merci, madame!*'

'There is just one thing,' she said, 'I have to open a garden fête on Saturday. They will expect me to be there.'

'That is okay!' he said graciously in English.

'I shall fetch my clothes from the house tonight,' she said. 'We can go to the fête from here, and when I have opened it I'll just vanish. We can't miss the evening rise on the trout stream, can we?'

'*Bien sûr, madame!*' said Robert.

Late that evening they crept into the house and came away with a suitcase packed with the Grandmère's dress, shoes and a triple string of pearls. 'I always open garden fêtes in pearls,' the Grandmère said. 'But I have never cooked sausages in them before!'

As they crept down the back stairs with a torch they heard a car entering the drive from the road.

'Run!' said the Grandmère. 'It's the family coming to see if I have got home. We mustn't be caught. Run!'

They ran, and were down the back drive and into the woods before the visitors had turned the last bend. The little Fiat was parked in some bushes opposite the back gate.

'You didn't lock the back door!' Robert said.

'Oh, they'll bang at the front. They'll never notice!' the Grandmère said. She wore her pearls to cook the sausages and they drank each other's health in Coca-Cola, calling themselves the New Outlaws.

'This is our last evening of liberty,' the Grandmère said on the next night, which was Friday. 'I am going to cook the best meal in the world in case we never come back again. Because once we get back into the ordinary world nothing will ever be quite the same again.'

She was very anxious to know if Robert had a clean shirt to wear at the garden fête, and it was while she was looking through his clothes that she remembered she had left her Fête-Opening-Hat behind her in the house. 'Why does it matter?' said Robert, but the Grandmère said she could not possibly open a garden fête without her proper hat on.

'I will fetch it for you!' Robert offered. He knew the way so well. He knew the house too, quite intimately, and it was not dark, and the Grandmère was very busy preparing the marvellous meal.

'Excellent!' she agreed. 'You don't even need a key.' And she told him where to find the hat. It sounded a very splendid kind of hat.

'Just bring it in your hands!' said Grandmère. 'But mind you wash them in the bathroom first!'

Robert went off through the woods as if the place belonged to him. With one ear cocked for bird song and the other for horses' hoofs he loped though the trees, remembering as if from long ago the weary pilgrimage in the rain that had led to his enchanting adventure. He knew now just where a pheasant was likely to start up, and where the first owl would wake. He jumped with delight when a badger lumbered away through the nettles, and cursed back under his breath when a jay swore at him. Once in the grounds of Grandmère's house he slipped through the sombre laurels at the back, and found the door unlocked as they had left it.

Robert had never been in Grandmère's house alone, but it had become so familiar that he was not afraid. He leapt lightly up the back stairs and down the long corridor to her bedroom. The hat was on the top shelf of her cupboard, Grandmère had said, in a deep blue box with a broken lid. He was to treat it carefully.

Robert did, but he was not tall, and he had to move several other boxes first. These, with the blue box on top, cascaded down on his head, and he had only time to salvage the hat before he heard the back door open and close downstairs, while voices and footsteps became louder and clearer as they mounted the back stairs.

The voices sounded like the voices of people who had every right to be in the house, not outlaws like himself. Who they could be he could not imagine, but he felt he had every reason to hide from them.

In a panic he dashed for the cupboard, but it was stuffed so full of boxes, dresses and bags of oddments that there was not a corner left for him to hide in. He flung himself down to look under the bed, but the weighty old-fashioned springs nearly touched the floor.

The footsteps had mounted the stairs now and were tramping along the corridor. The voices sounded as powerful as foghorns.

Robert leapt for the bed as his last hope of shelter. He dived under the silk coverlet, down under the matching eiderdown to the foot, where he lay as flat as he could spread himself. Somewhere on the way he lost hold of the hat, which sat in all its majesty on the Grandmère's pillow.

The footsteps came nearer. They did not even pause at the bedroom door but came right inside.

'Well I had a good look round last night, Sergeant, when I found the back door unlocked,' one voice said, 'and Police Constable Taylor has stayed round the place all day. We couldn't find nothing wrong.'

'Well look at that, then!' said the second voice grimly. It was a stern, superior voice, and Robert knew they were looking at the fumbled boxes. 'You didn't see *that*, I suppose?'

'Well no, Sergeant, we must have missed this room out!' said the first voice, sounding most guilty and unhappy. 'Funny, I thought we'd been everywhere, I really did, Sergeant!'

'Well, somebody has been having a high old time here,' the Sergeant said. 'Have a look where Mr Williams told you to look.

It's the pearls he was worried about. Never locked them up, he said . . . she just used to leave them about in her drawer. Go on . . . top left-hand drawer, in a velvet case . . . that's right, that's the case. . . .'

There was a terrible silence. Terrible, because Robert was scared clean out of his wits. 'Yes, they're gone all right!' said the heavier voice.

The next moment all the breath seemed to be pressed out of Robert's head. It was the police officer being knocked down as it were by a feather. He sat down heavily on the bed on top of Robert.

Robert would have suffered the crushing of a leg or an arm, but to have his head sat on was so like suffocation that he began to flail wildly with his legs and arms, with the result that the police officer sprang up with a yelp, while the Sergeant turned back the bedclothes and hauled Robert out of bed.

There was nothing he could say. Every word of English was scared clean out of him. He could not give his name, nor his address, nor any reason for his being there, and although he knew they were trying to make him say that he had not been the only person inside the house, he could not tell them that either. Because above all else he was not going to betray the Grandmère to anybody, least of all to the police.

'We had better take him down with us to the station,' the Sergeant said. 'Heaven knows how we get hold of his parents. The kid seems dumb. Perhaps one of the policewomen can cope.'

As they took him from the bed Robert made a last snatch at Grandmère's hat, but the police officer snatched it away again. They took him down the back stairs sobbing.

Before they reached the bottom they met someone coming up. It was Mr Williams.

'*Robert!*' Mr Williams exclaimed, and then: 'All right, officer, he's staying with my mother-in-law. He belongs to the house.'

The Sergeant dropped Robert like a hot brick.

'The pearls are gone, sir,' he said. 'And the bedroom is all upside down.'

Mr Williams pushed past them, leading Robert very kindly by the arm. He looked round the untidy bedroom in perplexity.

'Who did this?' he asked.

'*Moi.* I did it!' said Robert.

'Why? *Pourquoi?*'

'I was looking for the hat of madame.'

'And for her pearls?' broke in the Sergeant.

'Madame has her pearls *déjà* . . . already.'

'And where is madame now?'

Robert closed his mouth with a snap.

'Where is madame?'

'*Je ne sais pas.*'

'Nonsense!' For the first time Robert saw Mr Williams look angry. He took Robert's arm and shook it.

Robert pulled it away. Made fierce by indignation he dived under Mr Williams's elbow, past the policemen, out of the bedroom door, snatching up the Grandmère's hat from the chair where the Sergeant had carefully placed it.

Down the back stairs Robert ran, and out of the door. Under the laurels he slipped like a rabbit, cutting a long corner off the back drive. He dodged his way down to the road, crossed it, and was into the woods like a young animal that has escaped the hounds. Still he ran, and arrived at last quite breathless at the camping site, where Grandmère had just dished up the delicious supper she had prepared in his absence. She was wearing her pearls.

'We can do two things,' she said gravely, when he had finished his story. 'We can get into the car and go straight to the police station, or we can eat our supper and wait for the morning.'

'And catch the trout rise,' said Robert hopefully.

'Exactly,' said the Grandmère.

If the police did not discover them that evening nor the next morning it was because Mr Williams insisted that they should wait. So perhaps he was the only one not wholly astonished when shortly before 3 p.m. on the next afternoon Grandmère arrived in her little car, dressed in her most beautiful dress and pearls, crowned by her Fête-Opening-Hat, with Robert by her side, well-groomed and immaculately tidy, to open the garden fête. If both of them smelt faintly of wood smoke nobody said anything about it.

Grandmère was particularly charming to the Sergeant of police.

'We have been camping,' she explained. 'Yes, camping. In a tent.'

The Williams family welcomed Robert like a long lost brother.

Mrs Williams hugged him like a son. 'It was so clever of you to go off and find Grandmère all by yourself,' she said to him. 'But, oh dear! I was so anxious! Just until she telephoned to say you were there.'

He did not know how to explain to her so he went off and bought her an ice cream. Jenny and Sarah invited him to have tea in the gymkhana riders' tent with them, where they introduced him to most of their friends and all of the ponies. David, they said, was very nearly well again and Robert would be able to come home.

After tea he left the garden fête secretly with the Grandmère, joining her in the hidden place where she had put her car.

'We will finish the week-end out,' she told Robert as they drove at top speed towards their camping ground. 'And then we'll go back to the house and have baths and dress for dinner. And we'll go to the pictures every night until David is out of quarantine.'

'David is the only thing left to worry about,' sighed Robert. 'I am nervous about David.'

'David,' said Grandmère, 'is the nicest boy I have ever met except yourself, and you are both going to have a wonderful time when he goes back with you to France.'

'Perhaps,' said Robert, cheering up and looking more hopeful, 'we will be able to go camping.'

Wherever you go for the summer holiday or if you stay at home there is magic about. I think perhaps it starts with knowing how much free time you have. The other holidays are both short so you can see the end before they even start. It's not like that in the summer. Sometime in July the holiday will begin and far away in September—so far you can't bother about it—the holiday will end. In between, allowing for odd jobs, all the time is yours to do things, to see things, to plan things but, above all, to dream things.

Day dreams can be about anything: people you have read about that you would like to be, what you want to do when you grow up—just anything. For some of you—perhaps many of you—your day dreams take a shape in your mind and you feel you must write them down. Often the result is poetry—all sorts of poetry, lovely, imaginative, funny, it can take all shapes. Here is a funny poem with, I suppose, a moral for, as you will see, Elizabeth has seen an awful fate coming to poor Teresa, who quite possibly started on her downward—or should it be upward—path as a mere pencil chewer.

I have never met Elizabeth. All I can tell you about her is that she lives in Beckenham, which is part of Greater London, that she goes to school at Ravensbourne Grammar School, Nightingale Lane, Bromley. I can also add, having read this poem, that she has a nice sense of humour and a gift for humorous verse.

Teresa

This is the tale of Teresa Hood,
Whose common fault was chewing wood.
Breakfast, lunch, dinner and tea,
Her only cry and plea would be,
'Would that I could eat more wood,
That is the thing that does me good.'
One day she had a feast at school,
Pencils and pens and wooden rule.
Her teacher said, 'Now listen to me—
One day you'll turn into a tree.'
And sad to say the very next day,
Several branches made their way!
Slowly first, then quicker and quicker,
Shoots and twigs grew thicker and thicker!
And then one dreadful day she found,
Her feet were rooted to the ground!
Her face had gone I do declare,
Brown gnarled bark remained to stare.
Long golden locks were changing fast,
Until one day she found at last,
A jackdaw came to nest in them.
And made the greatest use of them.
And then one terrible day in spring,
Instead of hearing robins sing,

She heard a noise—a chippity chop,
And saw a tree nearby her, drop!
The wood-man came with his toothy saw,
And poor Teresa was no more!
So do not on your pencils dine,
You might change to an oak or pine!
Poor Teresa had an awful fate,
By turning into what she ate!

Elizabeth aged 12.

I do not suppose that Daphne du Maurier needs introducing to any of you. You may have seen revivals of some of her films, particularly Rebecca, *and you, who are older, will certainly have read her books. She is quite rightly one of the country's leading novelists, not only for the brilliance of her style but because she is a past mistress at the art of suspense. Oh, the hours she has kept me awake at night because I simply could not put a book of hers down.*

The name du Maurier was already famous when Daphne was born. Her grandfather was George du Maurier—one of the most distinguished artists ever to be a regular contributor to Punch. *He was also a playwright. One of his plays was called* Trilby *which many of you will have heard of, but as well she had an immensely distinguished father.*

Sir Gerald du Maurier, as he was to become, was a character you will seldom hear of today; he was an actor-manager and also a producer.

It is not easy for you to imagine what London theatres were like at the beginning of this century and up to the Second World War. There was so much glamour about them. The public looked upon going to the theatre as an occasion. Everybody sitting in the stalls or dress circle wore evening dress. Goodness knows what the front-of-the-house manager would have thought if he could see us slopping in today in just what we happen to have on.

Many of London's theatres were, in those days, leased to actor-managers who would run them for many years always providing the same sort of entertainment. Gerald du Maurier was one of the first of the naturalistic actors, that is, he appeared to be acting himself. Of course he was not, every move, every look and every inflection was planned and worked at and worked at. But his hard work was rewarded during his long lease of Wyndham's Theatre. He had success after success and the sort of plays he put on were called 'du Maurier plays'. All England in the period just before the First World War knew they could never go wrong if they bought tickets for Wyndham's. For they would see dear Gerald du Maurier, supported by a fine cast, and plays which would not upset the sensibilities of the most rigidly proper maiden aunt.

In the early days of Gerald du Maurier's climb to fame he was not married, and when he did marry and there were three baby girls in the nursery they of course knew nothing about the theatre. But babies grow up and in time the children were old enough to be taken to their father's first nights.

After Sir Gerald du Maurier died Daphne du Maurier wrote his biography. She called it Gerald: A Portrait. *It was a startling and brilliant piece of work, for few of us—even if we could write—would pretend to so intimate a knowledge of our fathers. There was in that book a description of the little du Maurier girls being taken to one of their father's first nights. I had always remembered it and when I was asked to edit this book I wrote to Miss du Maurier for permission to use the excerpt.*

DAPHNE DU MAURIER

Extract from Gerald: A Portrait

What triumphs they were, those opening nights at Wyndham's, with a play tuned to the highest pitch of perfection by diligent rehearsing, every member of the cast on his toes and at the top of his form, ready, like athletes in the pink of condition, to break records! They were nervous, of course—that was to be expected—and Gerald, coming home to an early dinner before the play, would show the strain by eating very little, by forcing his laughter, by humming just a shade too loudly the bars of a song.

Mo and the children, dressed in their best for the occasion, sat with flushed faces and wet hands, looking forward to the evening with mixed feelings, for by now they knew every line of the play as well as Gerald did himself; they knew just where it dragged, just where it was loose, and if somebody forgot his lines it would be greater agony than the dentist's chair. They drove down to the theatre in the car, and already a crowd had assembled on the pavement to watch the audience arrive. There was a whisper that turned into a shout when Gerald got out of the car—'There he is—there he goes'—and high-pitched exclamations as the family followed—'There she is—look, there are the children—oh, isn't she sweet—look at that one' and the du Maurier offspring followed their parents along the narrow alley-way that led to the stage door, scarlet with embarrassment, hiding their faces in their party cloaks. A wave of excitement met them as they entered the theatre; the very atmosphere was pregnant with emotion, and Tommy Lovell, the stage manager, smiled nervously, swallowing as though he had a bone in his throat, and rather bright about the eyes. Gerald's dressing-room was filled with flowers—from great monstrous emblems that topped the ceiling from acquaintances he had met at lunch, to the children's pot of heather on his dressing-table, and all manner of bulbs and pots and baskets, while telegrams fell from the table and slopped onto the floor. In the passage the call-boy shouted, 'Overture and beginners, please,' a haunting, fearful proclamation, a definite statement that escape was impossible and that the evening must be endured; and in a minute the first scrapings of the fiddles and the tap-tap of the conductor's stick could be heard, through the muffled barrier of the safety curtain, beyond the stage.

'You'd better get along to the box,' Gerald would say casually, as he put on his dressing-jacket and sat down before the mirror. The children would disappear, Mo hovering a moment to kiss him and wish him luck, and soon they had found their way to the box and were gazing down to the audience below, a great hum of excited chatter, laughter, and voices coming up to the box with a throbbing, unforgettable sound. Mo always sat well back screened by the curtain of the box from curious eyes, and Angela, the religious one of the party, was obviously praying in her corner, lips pressed together, hands tightly clasped. Daphne glowered sullenly at the stalls, hating everyone on sight, her eyes lighting for a second at the sight of her beloved Gladys Cooper; while Jeanne, newly promoted to the first-night status, beamed in appreciation upon the world in general, and waved a plump hand to the embarrassed staff from Cannon Hall, who returned the salutation meekly from the front row of the upper circle.

The orchestra blared its way to a conclusion, the programmes rustled, the doors were closed, the lights dimmed, the curtain rose suddenly with a swift and terrifying motion, and the play, for better, for worse, had begun.

Back in the dressing-room, Gerald was dressing for his part. He whistled softly between his teeth or hummed a little song. It was going to be all right, he knew that. His judgment had not

played him false. They had a real winner this time. But even with this belief there was an element of danger, a spark of uncertainty, that made the whole thing an adventure, an unbeatable thrill. One could never be entirely sure, and a first-night audience was a temperamental crowd, an unknown quantity. His heart beat a little more swiftly than usual, and his hands trembled as he lit his cigarette. 'Sir Gerald, please,' came the sing-song voice of the call-boy.

In less than three hours it would be over. The clapping would have died away. 'The King' would have been played, his speech of thanks delivered, the crowd of friends from the stalls would be flocking round to the buffet at the back of the stage, and he would be receiving congratulations from fifty people at a time, a glass of champagne in one hand and a sandwich in the other, while Tom Vaughan and Frank Curzon rubbed their hands in satisfaction and murmured in his ear, 'All right, Gerald, old man, you've done it again.' But now he was alone; this was his moment; this was his one little spark of adventure, the one time when he enjoyed acting, when it thrilled him, when, in spite of the nervousness and the strain, it meant anything at all.

I feel it is time we went abroad. Truly Robert in Ursula Moray Williams's story was French but I feel now we should move a really long way—to America.

John D. Fitzgerald is an American. He was born in Utah—where this next story is laid—and he lived there until he was eighteen. After that he went away to be a drummer in a band and he later became, amongst other things, a journalist.

It was his brother Tom who gave him the idea to write the book from which this story is taken. He called the book The Great Brain *and this story which he called 'The Last Chapter' is the end of the book. I have re-christened it* ANDY.

It was brother Tom who possessed the great brain. Always by thinking hard he could find solutions to every problem and all his solutions meant profit for himself, and always were very funny. In this story what is funniest does not concern Tom, it is the attempted suicide. You wait until you read about the mustang that will not cooperate. Do not forget, when you are reading this story, that it is laid in Utah at the beginning of the century, so you will find words that are strange to you, for instance, Sears Roebuck, where Andy's erector set came from, is a huge book for ordering by post. People still do their shopping through the Sears Roebuck catalogue to this day.

JOHN D. FITZGERALD

Andy

Our friend Andy Anderson didn't start to school with Tom and me that year. He had stepped on a rusty nail while playing in an abandoned barn on the outskirts of town a couple of weeks before school started. All the kids in town had been forbidden by their parents to play in the barn. What parents didn't seem to realize was that this was one sure way to make us kids play in the barn.

Andy knew he would get a whipping if he told his parents about stepping on the rusty nail. He kept the secret of his injured foot from his mother and father until blood poisoning had set in and turned into gangrene. By that time there was nothing else Doctor LeRoy could do but to amputate Andy's left leg just below the knee to prevent gangrene from spreading. I guess Tom missed Andy more than I did because he was nearer Andy's age, being just a year older.

It was the first week in November before Andy Anderson was able to attend school. Mr Jamison, the carpenter, had built a wooden peg leg for Andy with a pad made from leather where the knee rested.

At first all of us kids were quite awed by the peg leg. We tried it on and walked on it. But the novelty soon wore off and we began calling him Peg Leg. Andy couldn't join us in most of the games we played. His father must have realized this and had ordered an erector set from Sears Roebuck. I guess he thought the erector set would draw kids to the Anderson home where they would play with Andy. He was right. I learned from Howard Kay one Saturday morning that the erector set had arrived. We ran all the way to the Anderson home.

Andy came hobbling on his peg leg to the front door after we had rung the bell. Howard and I reminded him we were his friends. He invited us into the house and we played with the erector set until noon.

I told Tom about it as we sat on the front porch waiting for Mamma to call us for lunch.

'Gosh, T.D.,' I said, still filled with wonder. 'You never saw anything like it in your life. You can build windmills, steam shovels, cranes, and all kinds of things that actually work when you turn a crank.'

'I saw the picture of the set in the Sears Roebuck catalogue,' Tom said. 'It costs six dollars. If I had a set like that, I could make a fortune.'

'How?' I asked.

'By charging kids a cent an hour to play with it,' Tom answered. Then his face became thoughtful. 'Maybe I can work out a deal with Andy.'

'No, you can't,' I said. 'His father bought him the set so kids would play with Andy. You start charging and some kid will tell Andy's father.'

'I guess you're right,' Tom admitted. 'To heck with the erector set.'

The following Saturday afternoon Tom and I were on our front lawn with Andy when Sammy and the gang came along on their way to the Smiths' vacant lot to play One-O-Cat ball. Sammy had his ball and bat with him. Tom and I ran into the house to get our mitts.

Just as we came out the front door with our mitts, I saw Andy going around the corner of our house, I tossed my mitt on the front porch swing and followed him. I saw Andy walk around to the rear of our barn. I crept closer. Andy was sitting with his back against the barn. He had his arms across his knees, with his head buried on them. His shoulders were shaking. He was crying so hard it looked as if his whole body was trembling.

I didn't want him to know I'd been spying on him. I crept round to the front of the barn. I made a lot of noise entering it. Then I pushed the loose board aside at the rear and stepped out.

Andy was wiping his eyes with his sleeve. 'I thought you went to play ball,' he said as if he resented me being there.

'I changed my mind,' I said as I sat down beside him.

'Because you feel sorry for me,' he said with bitterness in his voice.

'Sure I feel sorry for you,' I said. 'But is it really so bad having a peg leg?'

'What good is a kid with a peg leg?' he asked hopelessly. 'I can't run and play with the other kids. I can't do my chores. It's like my Pa said. I'm plumb useless.'

'Your father said you were plumb useless?' I asked, unable to believe any father could be so cruel.

'He didn't know I heard him,' Andy said. 'I tried doing my chores for the first time when I got home from school yesterday. I got an armful of kindling from the woodshed. I fell trying to get up the back porch steps and spilled it. Then I dropped and spilled a bucket of coal. Then I tried to collect the eggs in the hen house and I dropped and broke them. Then Ma told me not to try to do any chores any more. And when Pa came home she told him. Pa didn't know I was on the back porch and could hear him and Ma in the kitchen. That was when he said they would have to take care of me the rest of my life because I was plumb useless.'

'I guess that makes you plumb useless all right,' I said.

'What's the use of me going on living when I'm plumb useless?' Andy asked.

'Not much,' I said, thinking how it would be if I couldn't play with other kids and my own father thought I was plumb useless.

'I'm going to do myself in,' Andy said desperately.

I couldn't help getting excited. 'You mean you are going to kill yourself?' I cried.

'Give me one good reason why not,' Andy said.

I thought and I thought and I thought but I couldn't think of one good reason. I was about ready to give up when I thought of the erector set.

'You are the only kid in town with an erector set,' I said, hoping that would cheer him up.

'What good is an erector set when I'm plumb useless like my Pa said?' Andy asked. Then he looked at me. 'Will you help me, John?'

I couldn't turn down a friend in need. 'Sure,' I promised.

'We've got to figure out a way to do myself in good and proper,' Andy said with a serious expression.

We discussed several ways for Andy to kill himself, only to discard them. I had never realized before what a problem it was for a person to figure out a way to kill himself. I was about to suggest we get Tom and his great brain to figure it out for us when I had an idea that sounded promising.

'I've got it,' I cried with excitement. 'How about hanging you?'

Andy's face broke into a grin. 'That is a peach of an idea,' he said.

'We'll hang you just like they hang outlaws,' I said.

'But I'm no outlaw,' Andy protested.

'You can pretend you are one can't you?' I asked.

'Why must I pretend to be an outlaw?' Andy wanted to know.

'Look, Andy,' I said a little exasperated with him, 'I promised Sweyn when he came to Salt Lake to school that I would take good care of his mustang Dusty. You don't think I'd let Dusty hang anybody who wasn't an outlaw, do you? It wouldn't be fair to Dusty. He's got to think he is hanging a sure enough outlaw.'

'All right,' Andy agreed. 'I'll pretend I'm an outlaw for Dusty's sake.'

We went into the barn. I got Sweyn's lariat and climbed up the rope ladder to Tom's loft. I tossed one end of the lariat over a rafter and let the rope slide down until Andy got a hold of it. I climbed down the rope ladder. I tied a slipknot noose on one end of the lariat. I handed the rope to him.

'Are you satisfied that is a good strong noose that won't come loose?' I asked.

Andy inspected the noose very carefully. 'I'm satisfied,' he said.

I put a halter on Dusty and led the mustang out of his stall to the side of a bale of hay. I helped Andy onto the bale of hay and from there to Dusty's back. I got some twine and stood on the bale of hay while I tied Andy's hands behind his back. Then I put the noose over Andy's head and pulled the slipknot until the noose was tight around his neck. I jumped down from the bale of hay and got the other end of the lariat. I tied it securely to a stall post. I stood back and looked at the lariat from the stall post to the rafter and back down to Andy's neck. It was tight. All was in readiness for the hanging.

'Dusty,' I said to the mustang, 'that isn't Andy Anderson on your back. That is the no good outlaw Peg Leg Andy you are about to hang.'

Dusty looked at me as if he understood. I walked around behind him.

'Are you ready to hang, you no good outlaw?' I asked Andy.

'Ready,' Andy replied. 'And before I go, John, I want you to know how much I appreciate you helping me to do myself in. You are a real pal.'

I took off my cap and raised my arm. I hit Dusty over the rump with my cap. I expected the mustang to jump and leave Andy dangling from the end of the lariat. Dusty didn't move. I hit him again with my cap and let out an Indian war cry at the same time. Dusty turned his head and looked at me with his ears flattened back, which meant he was angry. I hit him again with my cap and let out a real blood-curdling Indian war cry.

Dusty turned slowly around so Andy wouldn't fall off. He grabbed my cap out of my hand with his teeth. He dropped the cap by his forelegs and put a hoof in it. Then he twisted his head and rubbed his nose against Andy's good leg.

'He knows you because Sweyn let you ride him a few times,' I said. 'He knows you aren't an outlaw.'

'See if you can lead him,' Andy said. 'I ain't got all day.'

I took hold of the halter. I pulled on it. I begged Dusty to move. I coaxed him. I threatened him. All Dusty did was to flatten his ears back to let me know he was plenty angry at me.

'Try kicking him in the flanks,' I said to Andy.

Andy kicked Dusty in the flanks. At any other time Dusty would have bucked like crazy. But he didn't move an inch. His

ears got flatter and flatter as Andy kicked him in the flanks and I pulled on the halter.

'What the devil is going on here?' I heard Tom's voice behind me.

'I'm trying to hang an outlaw,' I said over my shoulder, 'but Dusty won't help me.'

'Stop it, you fool!' Tom shouted. 'You could kill Andy.'

'That is the idea,' I said as I continued to pull on the halter and Andy kept on kicking Dusty in the flanks. 'Andy is plumb useless with his peg leg and wants to do himself in. I'm his pal and I'm helping him.'

Tom grabbed the halter out of my hands. 'Steady, boy,' he said as he patted the mustang on the nose. 'Now, J.D.,' he said to me as he kept patting Dusty on the nose, 'untie the lariat from the stall post.'

I knew Dusty wasn't going to cooperate so I untied the lariat.

Tom let go of the halter. He took out his jack-knife and stepped on top of the bale of hay. He cut the twine I'd used to tie Andy's wrists. Then he loosened the noose and slipped the lariat over Andy's head. He then helped Andy down from the mustang. If he was expecting any thanks, he sure got a surprise.

'Why did you have to butt in?' Andy asked as tears came into his eyes.

Tom looked surprised all right. 'You mean you actually wanted to commit suicide and weren't just playing a game?' he asked, looking astonished.

'What good is a kid with a peg leg?' Andy sobbed as he sat down on the bale of hay and put his face in his hands. 'I can't play with the other lads. I can't do my chores. I'm plumb useless like Pa said and better off dead.'

'Nobody is plumb useless,' Tom said.

'A lot you know,' Andy cried. 'Even with your great brain you can't grow me another leg.'

'Of course I can't,' Tom admitted. 'But my great brain can prove to the world that you aren't plumb useless.'

For the first time since Andy had lost his leg I saw hope come into his eyes as he looked at Tom. 'If you can prove I'm not plumb useless to my Pa, I'll give you anything I've got,' he promised.

A cunning look spread over Tom's face. 'Even your erector set?' he asked.

Andy hesitated. 'I don't know if Pa would let me,' he said.

'What would your Pa do with the erector set if you committed suicide?' Tom asked. 'If you want to commit suicide or go on being plumb useless over an erector set, that is your business.' Tom started for the barn door.

'Wait, Tom!' Andy shouted. 'It's a deal.'

Tom turned around and walked over to the bale of hay. He held out his hand. 'Let's shake on it,' he said.

They shook hands to seal the bargain.

'I'll put my great brain to work on it right away,' Tom promised Andy. 'Meet me here after school starting Monday.'

After Andy left the barn to go home, Tom began to rub his hands gleefully. 'I'll make a fortune with that erector set, charging a cent an hour to play with it,' he said.

That evening after supper Tom sat staring into the burning log fire in the fireplace in our parlour for a long time before he got up and walked over to Papa.

'Papa,' he said, 'is it true that when a person loses an arm or leg, they get twice the strength in the other arm or leg?'

Papa laid aside a book he was reading. 'Perhaps not twice the strength, T.D.,' he said, 'but I have heard it said on good authority that a person does have more strength in the remaining limb. One theory is that it is a biological thing, and when a human body loses a limb, an organic change takes place which transfers more strength to the remaining limb. Another theory, and a much more logical one, is that when a person loses an arm or a leg, he will naturally use the remaining limb a great deal more, and this would of course strengthen that limb. I did know a one-armed miner in Silverlode who had twice the strength of a normal man in his one arm. I saw him perform feats of strength with that one arm that were amazing.'

'Thank you, Papa,' Tom said, smiling.

Tom and I were waiting in our barn Monday after school when Andy arrived. Tom put his hands on Andy's shoulders.

'Do you promise to put yourself in complete charge of my great brain and do everything I tell you to do?' he asked.

'I promise,' Andy said.

'Good,' Tom said. 'The first thing you've got to do is to stop feeling sorry for yourself.'

'I'll betcha you'd feel sorry for yourself if you had a peg leg,' Andy said.

'No, I wouldn't,' Tom said to my surprise, 'because I'd show every kid in town and my mother and my father that a peg leg didn't make any difference. We will start by proving you can play any game as good as a kid with two legs. We'll start with Duck on a Rock.'

I helped Tom carry two flat slabs of rock into the barn and place them ten paces apart. We put a round rock about the size of a baseball on each slab. We laid six round rocks about the size of a baseball near one of the slabs. Tom picked one up. The idea of the game was to knock the rock representing the duck off the slab. Tom threw and hit the duck, knocking it off. I ran to put it back.

Andy then made an underarm pitch and missed the slab by three feet.

'It's no good,' he said, discouraged. 'I can't balance myself right with this peg leg.'

'Take it off,' Tom said.

I watched Tom strap the peg leg to his left knee. Tom took a few steps around on the peg leg. Then he tried pitching rocks at the duck on a rock with his left leg in front of him. Then he tried pitching with his right leg in front of him.

'You get off balance,' Tom said to Andy, 'when you put the peg leg in front and bring your weight down on it when you pitch.'

'But that is the way I pitch,' Andy protested. 'I can't pitch with my right leg in front.'

'Of course you can,' Tom said. 'Now watch me.'

Tom took a pitch. He missed the duck on a rock but did hit the slab. He took off the peg leg and handed it to Andy.

'Now we'll play,' Tom said. 'The first one to knock the duck off the rock ten times is a winner.'

The first game Tom got ten ducks before Andy knocked off even one. The second game Andy improved. He got two ducks before Tom knocked off ten. They kept at it until it was time for Andy to go home. During the last game Andy knocked off five ducks before Tom got ten.

'Practice makes perfect,' Tom said as we came out of the barn. 'We'll keep at it until you can hold your own with any kid in town.'

The next afternoon after school when Andy met us in the barn, his face was thoughtful.

'I wish you'd do something about my chores,' he said to Tom. 'My Pa is going to think I'm useless as long as he has to do my chores for me.'

'I guess that is more important than learning how to play games with your peg leg,' Tom said. 'We'll spend half our time each day teaching you how to do your chores and the other half teaching you how to play games. Now, why can't you do your chores?'

'Well, gee,' Andy said, 'you know I've got a peg leg.'

'Answer the question,' Tom said.

'Well, for one thing, I can't get up and down the back porch steps without holding onto the railing with one hand. So I can't carry an armful of kindling which you have to hold with both hands. And bucketfuls are so heavy I have to lift them up the steps with both hands. And I wobble so much I can't carry a pail of milk without . . .'

'That's enough,' Tom interrupted him. 'Let's go to our back porch.'

We walked to the steps of our back porch.

'Show me how you go up and down the steps,' Tom ordered Andy.

Andy took hold of the railing and walked up and down the steps.

'Take off the peg leg and let me try it,' Tom said. 'You try to go up and down as if you had two good legs. When you put the peg leg up first, you have to pull yourself up by holding onto the railing.'

Tom strapped on the peg leg. 'Now watch me,' he said.

He put his right foot on a step and using his right leg lifted his body up, bringing the peg leg up beside his right leg. 'There is nothing to it,' he said. 'Let your right leg do all the work.'

Andy watched bug-eyed as Tom went up the rest of the steps without holding onto the railing.

'Now I'll come down,' Tom said.

He tried putting his right foot down first and lost his balance. He had to grab the railing to keep from falling.

'It worked going up,' Tom said.

Again he tried putting his right foot down first. Again he lost his balance. He sat down on the steps.

'If it works going up, why won't it work going down?' he asked as if talking to himself. 'You fellows be quiet. I've got to put my great brain to work.'

Andy and I remained quiet. I knew Tom's great brain was working like sixty as I watched wrinkles come into his forehead. Suddenly the wrinkles disappeared. Tom was smiling as he stood up.

'I used my good leg to lift my body going up,' he said. 'I made the mistake of trying to use the peg leg to lift my body going down. Now watch this.'

Tom balanced himself on his right leg, holding his weight as he put the peg leg down a step. Then he stood on the peg leg for just a second while he quickly brought his right foot down a step. He came like that all the way down the steps without losing his balance. He took off the peg leg and handed it to Andy.

'You saw me go up using my right leg to lift my body and you saw me coming down using my right leg to lift my body,' he said. 'Now you try it.'

Andy strapped on the peg leg. He had no trouble going up but lost his balance coming down.

'It's harder to come down,' Tom said, 'but don't get discouraged. All it takes is practice.'

Tom made Andy practise going up and down the steps for an hour.

The next afternoon after school Tom and I were waiting for Andy on the steps of our back porch. Again Tom made Andy go up and down the steps for an hour. Andy got so he could practically run up and down the steps without holding onto the railing.

The next afternoon Tom's face was thoughtful as he waited for Andy. 'You know, J.D.,' he said to me, 'I think it is time for Andy to learn how to carry things up and down the steps. And to make sure he can do his chores to please his father, I think I'll start letting him do ours.'

When Andy arrived, my brother led him to the woodshed. 'We are going to start practising real chores today,' Tom said. 'We'll begin by letting you fill all the wood boxes in our house with kindling wood.'

Andy looked so happy I didn't have the heart to tell him that he was being taken. With a big happy grin on his face he carried a big armful of kindling wood from our woodshed, up the steps, into the kitchen and dumped it into the wood box by the kitchen range.

'What is this all about?' Mamma asked.

'I'm teaching Andy how to do his chores,' Tom said proudly.

Aunt Bertha just shook her head. 'Oh, that boy,' she said.

I watched as Andy filled the woodboxes for the fireplace, the pot-bellied stove in the dining-room, and the stove in the bathroom.

'Now for the coal buckets,' Tom said as we came out of the kitchen carrying empty coal buckets. Then I guess my brother's conscience bothered him a bit. 'No hurry, Andy,' he said. 'Take a rest first if you want.'

Andy still had that happy grin on his face. 'I don't need a rest,' he said. 'Let's go.'

After Andy had filled all the coal buckets in our house, I thought that was enough for one day. But not Tom.

'I'd let you do the milking,' Tom said, 'but I'm afraid you

might spill it carrying it. So, we'll spend the rest of the day practising.'

Tom got a milk pail and filled it full of water at the hydrant. 'Now I want you to practise carrying this to the barn and back until it is time for you to go home.'

Andy spilled half the water out of the bucket the first trip as Tom and I watched.

'No wonder your father won't let you bring in the milk,' Tom said. 'Give me that bucket.'

My brother filled the pail with water. Then he strapped on the peg leg. He picked up the pail of water and started to walk. He spilled water all over.

'Now watch, J.D.,' he said, 'and tell me if the water spills when I'm on my right leg or the peg leg.'

I watched as Tom started to walk. The water spilled when he tried to step on the peg leg. I told him so.

'It's because I'm trying to take a natural step,' he said. 'Now I'm going to take a little short step with the peg leg to help me keep an even balance.'

He looked funny taking a little short step with the peg leg and a big step with the right leg, but he didn't spill a drop. He removed the peg leg and made Andy put it on while he filled the pail to the brim with water

'Now do like you saw me do,' he said to Andy. 'A little short step with the peg leg and a natural step with the good leg.'

Tom made Andy practise until it was time for Andy to go home.

'Can I start doing my chores at home tomorrow?' Andy asked as if excited.

'No,' Tom said. 'You need at least another week of practice. We don't want to take any chances your father won't be completely satisfied.'

Tom made Andy do all our chores for a whole week before he announced Andy could do his own chores starting the following day.

It was a proud day for Andy when he reported he had done all the chores he used to do at home before he lost his leg.

'I brought in the kindling and the coal,' he said when he met us at school. 'I slopped the pigs without spilling any of the slop from the buckets. I carried the milk in without spilling a drop. I fed the chickens and collected the eggs. I went to the store for Ma and carried everything home without dropping anything. Pa says he is proud of me. I guess he doesn't think I'm plumb useless any more.'

'You are still useless as a kid,' Tom said. 'What good is a kid who can't run? If you can't run, you can't play a lot of games. Meet me in our corral after school and I'll start teaching you to run.'

'I can't stay late any more,' Andy said. 'I've got my chores to do now.'

'We'll only spend half an hour a day on school days,' Tom said.

Andy walked home from school with Tom and me. I knew my brother had a great brain, but trying to teach a kid with a peg leg to run was beyond my imagination. I was curious as all get out as we entered the corral.

Tom ordered Andy to run round the corral. Andy tried to run but kept falling down. Then Tom strapped on the peg leg. He had no better luck than Andy and kept falling down.

'There must be some way of doing it,' he said, undaunted. 'Tomorrow is Saturday. Meet me here tomorrow afternoon. I'll put my great brain to work on it and figure out a way to make you run.'

The next morning Tom and I did all our chores and then Mamma kept finding other things for us to do. We didn't get a chance to even sit down and rest until just before lunch. We were sitting on the swing on our front porch. We were watching Irene Olsen and Christine Mackie playing hopscotch across the street. Tom suddenly snapped his fingers.

'That's it!' he shouted.

'What?' I asked.

'My great brain has figured out a way to make Andy run!' he said, grinning.

'How?' I asked, wondering how a kid with a peg leg could ever learn to run.

'You'll see this afternoon,' Tom said mysteriously.

We ate lunch and then went to meet Andy in our corral. He arrived a few minutes later.

'Give me that peg leg,' Tom said.

Tom strapped on the peg leg.

'Now watch this!' he shouted.

I burst out laughing as Tom took a hop, skip, and jump on his right leg and then a step on the peg leg. It was like watching a man run on three legs and looked very comical. He fell down a few times but kept on trying until he'd run all the way across the corral and back without even stumbling.

'Now you try it,' Tom said to Andy as he unstrapped the peg leg.

An hour later and Andy was ready to give up. He kept falling down when he tried to run.

'I'm no good,' he said, 'and besides my knee hurts.'

'How do you think my knee feels?' Tom demanded as he rolled up his pants leg and showed us a knee that was turning black and blue. 'My great brain has figured out a way to make you run and you're going to learn how to run. Now try it again.'

A week later Andy was singing a different tune. Tom had made him practise running every day.

'Today,' Tom said as we entered the corral, 'you are going to race J.D. across the corral and back and you are going to beat him.'

'I'll beat him,' Andy said confidently.

Andy and I got on our marks and got set. Tom gave the signal. I beat Andy across the corral but I had to slow down to turn round. Andy just spun around on his peg leg without slowing down and beat me back to the starting line.

'You can now run well enough to play any game,' Tom announced.

'I can't play ball,' Andy said.

'Why not?' Tom asked.

'Because I can't bat with a peg leg,' Andy explained.

'We'll fix that,' Tom said.

And fix it he did. Within a week he had Andy batting better with a peg leg than Andy could ever bat with two legs. Tom discovered that Andy shut his eyes when he took a swing at the ball. As soon as he trained Andy to keep his eyes on the ball, Andy began whacking Tom's pitches all over the corral.

The following Saturday Tom suggested we all go into our backyard and play Duck on a Rock. Only four could play at a time. Tom chose Andy for his partner. Sammy chose Danny Forester as his partner for the first game. Tom and Andy beat Sammy and Danny. Then they beat Basil and Jimmie and finally had no trouble beating Pete Kyle and me.

'Let's change partners this time,' Sammy suggested. 'I'll take Andy for my partner.'

I don't know if my brother tried his best or not but Andy and Sammy knocked off ten ducks to eight ducks for Tom and Danny and won the game. Then Sammy and Andy beat Basil and Jimmie and then clobbered me and Pete.

'I've had enough of this game,' Tom said. 'Let's play Kick the Can.'

'Why not play something Andy can play?' Sammy asked.

'What makes you think he can't play Kick the Can?' Tom asked.

'He can't run on his peg leg,' Sammy said.

'We always let J.D. play,' Tom said. 'If Andy can beat him running, it means he can play.'

'Sure,' Sammy agreed, 'but how can Andy run on a peg leg?'

Tom pointed. 'They will race to the end of the alley and back to the woodshed.'

We all went into the alley, where Andy and I got on our marks.

'One for the money,' Tom chanted, 'two for the show, three to get on your marks, and off you go.'

I ran as fast as I could, but Andy beat me back to the woodshed by ten feet.

'Gosh, Peg Leg,' Sammy said, patting Andy on the shoulder, 'you were just great. I would never have believed it if I hadn't seen it with my own eyes.' He began laughing. 'You looked funny as the devil, but how you can run.'

The other kids all congratulated Andy. We played Kick the Can until it was time for lunch. I had to run an errand for Mamma after lunch. I ran all the way to the Smith's vacant lot after the errand where I knew the kids were meeting to play baseball. Tom and Sammy had just finished hands over fists on Sammy's bat. Tom had won and got first choice in choosing up the two teams to play. Sammy didn't even look surprised when Tom chose Andy first. I guess after what had happened that morning Sammy wouldn't have been surprised if Andy had run and jumped over our barn.

It had taken Tom and his great brain four weeks to prove Andy wasn't useless and could hold his own in any games we kids played. I'd forgotten about the erector set until after supper that evening. Andy came to our front door carrying the set under his arm. He asked Tom to come out on the front porch. I followed.

'Here is the erector set like I promised,' Andy said. 'I told my Pa all you did for me. I told him how you showed me I could still do my chores with my peg leg. I told him how you helped me so I could play games with the kids with my peg leg. I told him how you made me feel I was no longer useless. I told him how I would have killed myself if it hadn't been for you. I told him how you made me want to go on living. And I told him I had promised you the erector set if you could prove to him and to me I wasn't useless any more. Pa said it was all right to give it to you.'

It was at that moment in my brother's life when he was suddenly attacked by a strange disease which completely paralysed his great brain and he didn't know what he was saying or doing. At least that is what I thought when Tom didn't snatch the erector set out of Andy's hands.

'It is true,' Tom said modestly. 'My great brain saved you from a suicide's grave. It is also true I proved to you and your Pa that you weren't useless. And it is true we made a deal and I have more than lived up to my end of the bargain. But it just doesn't seem right somehow for me to take the erector set.'

Andy's eyes got wide. 'Don't you want it?' he asked, hugging the set to his chest.

'Of course I want it,' Tom answered, 'but it just doesn't seem right getting paid for helping somebody not to be useless any more. You keep the set, Andy. I'll come over and play with it sometimes.'

It is a dream, I told myself. I watched Andy press his lips together as tears bubbled up in his eyes.

'You can play with the set any time,' he said. 'And my Pa said to thank you for him. My Ma said God bless you and she would pray for you. Ain't no way for me to say what I feel inside for you making me so I'm not useless any more. I guess I'll just have to thank you in my prayers and ask God to bless you.'

Andy walked to our front gate. I could see tears streaming down his cheeks as he turned to wave at us. I knew they were tears of happiness and gratitude as I watched him go whistling down the Main Street with the erector set under his arm.

Things got mighty dull after The Great Brain decided to give up his crooked ways and to walk the straight and narrow. So dull Papa didn't even bother to come upstairs and see if Tom was in bed the night the school-house burned down. So dull there is no more to tell.

The next story takes us back to England, not England today but as it was perhaps hundreds of years ago. The subject of the story is treasure trove. Actually the treasure Victoria found did not belong to England but how did it get to where it was found? How long had it been in England and to whom did it belong?

This story introduces you to a fascinating hobby. It is to become a collector. Many of you already will have arrowheads and pieces of pottery you have picked up somewhere, and holding them in your hand have wondered about the people who made them and used them. But treasure need not be very old. If you could find treasures that belonged to your great-grandmother or grandfather you would probably be surprised at how much they would tell you about the way they lived.

Those of you who were lucky enough to be taken to see the Tutankhamun exhibition when it was in London must have felt a feeling almost of having known the boy when you looked at the things he had touched and used. His lighter, not so unlike a lighter today, that he cherished so much it was buried with him. The little chair on which he sat when he was small. The game he enjoyed playing with his child wife. So like in many ways things a small boy might treasure today and yet all over 3,000 years old.

Of course all treasure hunters cannot be winners, but it's an idea to start collecting. So wherever you are begin searching and perhaps, like Victoria in the story, you might be lucky.

DOROTHY CLEWES

Lost Treasure

'Do we have to have this programme?' Simon asked. The man on TV was talking about ancient relics. He talked about them once a week—in a programme called 'Lost Treasures', and always Victoria turned on the set to listen to him. Simon couldn't imagine what she saw in it. There was a Western on the other channel and they all liked Westerns—even Julia who at fourteen considered herself too old for them, and Pete who was seven and the baby.

'Westerns are on all the time,' Victoria said. 'This programme is only once a week and this is the last but one in the series. Besides, it's my turn to choose the programme.'

The television set had been a present from the school when their father had died last year. It had been a generous gesture from the Governors on top of the not-so-generous pension which their mother received, and it kept them occupied and entertained, as it was meant to do, while their mother was out in the evening, as she now so often had to be.

'He looks like an ancient relic himself,' Simon said.

'Well, you don't have to look if you don't want to,' Julia said, though secretly agreeing with him. Busy altering a summer frock that had belonged to her mother she was glad not to be involved in anything except the job in hand. She had never owned an absolutely new frock, always they had belonged to a cousin who was her own age but a bit fatter—and the way things were it didn't look as if she ever would. It was very depressing.

'He's a famous professor,' Victoria said, indignantly. 'All professors look like that.' She was sure they didn't, but this was the first she had ever seen and it was the way they ought to look. 'It's because they're interested in—in *deeper* things,' she said.

The professor had a little pointed beard, rumpled hair, and thatch-like eyebrows, but under the eyebrows the eyes were serious and kind.

'You mean the things they dig up are deeper down in the earth,' Simon said. He couldn't help teasing Victoria: she took everything so seriously, especially this silly programme.

'No, I didn't mean that,' Victoria said, solemnly. 'I meant—deeper *spiritually*.' She knew they all thought she was odd, and perhaps she was: at twelve she felt older than any of them, even older than Mummy.

'Aren't we going to have the Wethtern?' Pete piped through the gap left when his two front teeth had come out. It made him sound like a baby, but however carefully he spoke he couldn't make the 'ss' come out properly.

'Haven't you gone to bed yet?' Julia said, but there was no weight behind her words. She had hated being sent to bed when she was seven. Now, when she was nearly always late she would have liked to go to bed early—but there was always so much to do: the last hot drinks to make, hot water bottles to be filled, the table to be laid for breakfast—and if Mummy was out, sitting up until she came in because she knew how much Mummy hated coming in to a silent house.

'*Now* you can have the Western,' Victoria said, as the kindly, smiling face of the professor was faded out with his last words: '. . . so remember, if you have any treasures, let me have them at this address and I will be glad to talk about them. . . .' The picture faded into the caption carrying the address, and Victoria stretched out and turned the control knob to the other channel. The sheriff had got his man: he lay biting the dust of the shanty-town street, his bullying over—until next week.

'It's finished,' Pete wailed.

'And now it *is* time you went to bed,' Julia said. 'And you too, Victoria.'

But Victoria wasn't listening. She was still hearing the voice of the professor: '. . . so remember, if you have any treasures, let me have them at this address and I'll be glad to talk about them. . . .'

If only one of her treasures was worth *talking* about. And if she had anything worth talking about it might be worth selling. They wanted money so badly. Mummy needed a holiday. They

all needed a holiday, but Mummy most of all. It had been like this ever since Daddy died and Mummy had had to go back to her original job of teaching—at the school. When evening work came up in the shape of extra coaching—as it had done tonight—she couldn't afford to turn it down.

'Bed', Julia said again, and this time got some action.

In the bedroom she shared with Julia, Victoria gazed around her: at least around her half of the bedroom: the half where the shelves were. It was the shelves she was looking at. They held all her treasures, neatly labelled and evenly spaced—from the coloured stones she had picked up on the beaches at the seaside, to the polished shell of a tortoise that had once been a pet. She took up the silver buckle her mother had given her from her own box of treasures: Grandmother, 1890, the label read. And the cartridge case she had dug up from the garden. Daddy had dated that for her: London, 1943. She had polished it until it shone like a miniature golden temple. And there was the copper coin which she had found herself, and which could have been old but was probably only very worn, the date having been rubbed off and most of the impression, too. And the bone. It was a large bone, and took up a lot of room on the shelf.

'A meat bone! Really, you must be batty,' Julia had said. 'The dustbin is the place for old bones, not a collector's shelf.' But Victoria had kept the bone because—well, because it was a nice shape, and in her hand it *felt* nice. She couldn't explain it any better than that. She had found it on the same old bomb site where she had found the coin and had labelled it: Bomb site. London, 1965. Workmen had been clearing the site and now a large block of flats stood on the spot.

Victoria sat on the edge of her bed and tried to make up her mind whether to do what she had been thinking. Clutter, Julia had called her treasures—and perhaps it was, Victoria sighed. But at least the buckle was nice—and perhaps much older than Mummy thought. It might have been handed down to Granny by her Granny, and from lots of other Grannies before that. It might be worth *something*. And any one of the stones could at least be semi-precious.

Her mind suddenly made up, Victoria rummaged in her cupboard and brought out a boot box. Into it she swept all the treasures, and then sat down to write the letter which she would send with it. She remembered the address because it came on the screen after every programme, and when she had tied up her parcel, she printed it in large black letters on the wrapping paper. The postage took all her pocket money, but with the parcel on the other side of the post-office counter, she did not like to ask for it back.

'Well—and about time, too,' Julia exclaimed when she saw the empty shelves. 'Now you can collect something really nice: little pieces of china. Look'—handing her a miniature jug from her own side of the bedroom,—'you can have this for a start.'

The little jug was beastly, Victoria thought: it had a lot of painted flowers on it in hard colours, and in the middle, in a heart-shaped space was written the words: 'A Present from Brighton', but she took it and put it on one of the shelves because she didn't want to talk about her lost treasures which Julia thought she had thrown away.

The week dragged itself by. Victoria tried hard not to think what might be happening to the box of treasures. It was so easy to imagine what *could* have happened to it. When she closed her eyes she could see the professor *and* the box. She could see him tearing off the wrapping paper, lifting the lid—and gazing down at the contents in amazement. Then, the first shock over, throwing back his head and roaring with laughter, and then all the other people in the studio gathering round and laughing, too, holding up the silver buckle, the coin and the cartridge case, and turning over the stones—until they found the bone, and that would set them off again. At night Victoria hid her head under the bedclothes trying to shut out the picture, but she could only see it all plainer than ever.

'We haven't got to have the beathly Pwofethor again, have we?' Pete wailed, when at last the day for the programme arrived.

'Yes,' Julia said, suddenly asserting her authority. She didn't know why Victoria had suddenly thrown away all her treasures, and making sure that she saw the programme was the only way she could think of saying she was sorry. 'You know this is a programme Victoria specially likes. After tonight you can have Westerns all the time.'

Victoria could hardly bear to look at the tiny screen—and at the same time she could not take her eyes away from it. A voice was speaking, announcing the programme, and immediately, like magic, there was the professor. On the table in front of him there was a Roman helmet, an earthenware water bottle, and something that looked like a scythe—but no boot box, no stones, no bones, no silver buckles. Victoria did not know whether to be glad or sorry. How *could* she have thought her treasures had any value when measured against such spectacular things as helmets, and remains of a pre-Roman scythe which had been sent in from someone in the North of England and about which the professor was now talking. And listening to the professor Victoria forgot her own box of treasures and was back in those ancient times, working with the peasants in the fields, wielding the rough scythe in the clearing of their patch of land. She was still centuries away long after the professor had returned to here and now. She hadn't heard the start of what he was saying, but suddenly she was aware of his voice, of the words he was speaking:

'. . . and all treasures are not as old as these we have been talking about. A parcel came to me the other day and contained one of those rare shocks of surprise that we all dream about but which occur all too seldom.' His hand reached into a drawer of the desk he was sitting at, and came up with—the boot box. *Her* boot box. Victoria's heart pounded. It couldn't be true. All boot boxes looked alike—and then the professor was speaking her name.

'Victoria, if you are watching this programme and I hope you are—I want first of all to thank you for letting me see your treasures——' His hand was holding the silver buckle, and now Pete and Simon and Julia were gasping, too, questioning her, but Victoria could only hear the professor's voice. 'The buckle is a pretty Edwardian piece of costume decoration. Not of any value now, but if it is preserved and lives to be as old as the pieces I have just been showing you it will have interest and value for people who come after us. And the stones——' He put the buckle down and brought out the coloured stones, put those down on the desk and brought out the cartridge case. 'Inanimate objects speak,' he said. 'Never forget that. Think what story this will tell many years from now: a German bullet——' He was reading the stamping on the base of the cartridge—'found on London soil in the year 1943. But——' He put down the cartridge and put his hand into the boot box again. 'I wonder, Victoria, if you realized the value of this other treasure of yours.' There wasn't a sound in the room, now. Pete, Simon and Julia might have been inanimate objects themselves, they were so still. 'I can't tell you its full worth,' the professor went on, 'but it is in the region of several hundreds of pounds,'—and with that he drew out—the meat bone.

'From your label, Victoria, I don't think you have any idea what you found on that bomb site in the year 1965. Maybe the owner of it can be traced, but I think that very unlikely. This very beautiful piece of South African ivory—from the tusk of some mighty elephant—although its tip has at one time been cut off, or broken off, is still worth a great deal of money. I would like, if I may, to return this to you myself——'

The bone! Among the clamour of voices, only Julia's was silent. If she had had her way the bone would have gone into the dustbin. She had made fun of Victoria's hobby: they had all made fun of it—but Victoria had *known*.

'No, I didn't,' Victoria was assuring them all, 'but there was something about it. I liked the *look* of it, the *shape* of it, and the *feel* of it——' Perhaps when the professor came he would explain. There were other things she would like him to explain, too: how she could learn to *recognize* treasures, real treasures.

'I know it's your money,' Simon was beginning to say,—and there was a note of respect in his voice. Old Victoria, who'd have thought it——?

'It's *our* money,' Victoria corrected him because Simon's thought was in all their minds. 'Now we can have that holiday, and Mummy can have some fun again—and you can have a new dress, Julia, really new and all your own. And you, Simon, and Pete—anything you want.' Victoria sighed happily. There was nothing she wanted for herself: nothing except to be allowed to go on looking for lost treasures: not necessarily ones that were worth a lot of money, but treasures that spoke to you, that told you all about families like themselves who had lived many, many years ago.

Although this next story is about Christmas I have put it in this summer book because it is about a hot Christmas.

Rumer Godden lived in India when she was a child, so this story is something she remembers. It is a memory with which I can sincerely sympathize for I too had 'giving away' thrust upon me so I know how it feels. Not that we had to give away new things which not only had we never touched but longed to own, as did Rumer Godden, but we were expected to share what we had with those poorer than we were. I do not think we minded when we were asked what we wanted to give away. What we resented was when some grown-up chose what we should be parted from.

Reading Rumer Godden's description of her long-ago Christmases I wished so much she could just once have had a 'dolly' all to herself.

RUMER GODDEN

Loving and Giving

'Christmas is a time for giving as well as getting.' Every child knows that; even two and three year olds are initiated into secret buyings and wrapping ups; all autumn, children spend hours in making things, those heavy-as-lead carpentry gifts (mother and father paying for the wood), raffia mats, cross-stitch kettle-holders, embroidery, home bound books. 'You must not only give, you must love to give,' our mother insisted, and in spite of the work it was easy to love this planning and spending; but when it came to giving away our *own* presents, presents we had been given, it was quite another idea and in our Indian childhood it seemed exceedingly hard that we, four sisters, were never allowed to keep a single thing from any of the Christmas 'dollies'.

A 'dolly'—I must explain—was not a doll; it was the name given to the baskets of gifts brought on Christmas morning by Indian merchants, contractors and head members of the office staffs as compliments to their Christian clients and employers.

It had become a custom, and custom had built up a ritual for it. The dollies were not handed over in the offices; they were presents and had to be presented with Indian courtesy which meant that every giver had to call personally at each house and make his salaams.

For the merchants and babus it must have been an arduous and expensive morning—for us it was a training in patience and obedience. My father and mother received on the front verandah; Mahommed Shah, our big Mahommedhan butler, regulated the queue, announcing each visitor in turn. Perhaps it would be one of my father's own babus resplendent in snow white muslin shirt and dhoti—the long flowing cloth worn draped as a nether garment—coloured socks and sock suspenders, patent leather pumps; perhaps it was a Marwari, one of the merchants or stockbrokers, usually rich and dressed in a cream silk achkan—a long tunic coat—marigold-coloured turban, a fresh scarlet tika mark on his forehead. A tika mark is the small red spot painted between the eyebrows, put on by the priest after ritual bathing. Sometimes a Marwari would bring his children, they were in European clothes except for round velvet hats like pill-box lids embroidered in gold. They had gold earrings too, and smelled strongly of coconut oil. At once an unspoken bond would spring up between us and them—the dolly things were not for them either.

The ritual was always the same: my father was garlanded, sometimes my mother; in a minute or so the long necklaces of jessamine or marigold flowers would be taken off and coiled on a tray held by Abdul, our officious nursery servant—Abdul had always to be in on everything—and as the morning went on the pyramid of garlands grew into a scented mountain. The caller was seated and five minutes would be spent in polite conversation. We children were not often brought into the foreground or the conversation—my father and mother had no son and the calamity of four daughters, all of whom would presumably have to be dowried, was better ignored—but there was plenty to interest us; during the talk, the baskets were carried in by the caller's servants and put down at my father's feet.

Dollies were always in light round baskets, of the sort coolies use, but now decorated with flowers and sheets of coloured paper. Sometimes there was only one, sometimes two or three, their number and cost depending on the richness of the giver, and the importance of my father's patronage to him; sometimes it was in genuine gratitude for help in the past year, but the giver knew, as my father knew—as everyone in India knew—that there was a code of strict limitation on the cost.

In the old East India Company days dollies were often bribes—and fabulous bribes. This suspicion of bribery still hung over them and anything gold or silver, even children's bangles, was immediately handed back; there could be none of the exquisite gauze and gold thread saris or scarves that came from Benares; a bottle of whisky or a length of plain silk was the utmost limit. Usually there were only flowers, fruit, cakes, sweets and, for us children, crackers and toys.

In spite of the semi-royal state in which the English in India lived, we were brought up quite frugally, not too much of anything, certainly not many toys and we yearned after those dollies. Certainly, I have never seen anything more attractive: the foundation was always fruit; red apples from Kulu, bananas—sometimes a whole stem of them was carried in and set beside the basket as an extra—papayas, pommelloes like big pink fleshed grapefruit, tangerines in silver paper, nuts. To one side would be a Christmas cake, florid with shop icing, which we thought wonderful—our cake was home made. There would be a box of chocolates tied with ribbon—sometimes four boxes of chocolates for four sisters, never to be allowed to keep them. There were Indian sweets, jillipis, clear spiral rings of toffee sugar—or sandesh, which was a sort of fudge stuck with silver paper. Crackers and toys were poised on top. We duly had to thank for them; the caller airily waved his hand and said 'They are nothing, nothing,' though they must have cost him many rupees. He then made way for the next visitor and the baskets were spirited away.

Not entirely spirited. They were taken to the dining-room, which in our Indian built home was as large as a ballroom; there Nan, our Eurasian nurse, and our Ayah, unpacked them and arranged them on the dining-room table in pyramids of fruit, platters of sweets, rows of cakes, piles of crackers; the toys were heaped on the floor. As soon as the last caller had gone from the front verandah, the last car or tikka gharri—little box-like carriages drawn by two ponies—driven away, a familiar, shuffling, rustling, whispering, giggling and sniffling began on the back verandah. The noise grew louder until Mahommed Shah threw open the door and in came the droves of the servants' children.

We were not rich people but we must have had something like eighteen servants then, Christian, Mahommedhan, Hindus of all castes and there were between sixty and eighty children including the dhobi's (washerman's) clan, now mysteriously swelled to double size—but my mother never sent any of the little gate-crashers away. Some we knew well as they lived in the compound; some, like Mahommed Shah's, who had a house nearly as large as ours, came only at Christmas. Some were our enemies—there had been scuffles and ambushes—some our dear friends, but now one would have thought we had never met before; we of the back verandah were quite as ceremonious as our elders of the front. There were, of course, no garlands but the children gave us salaams which we gravely returned.

The protocol was strict: Mahommed Shah's big girl and small boys stood near the table—they in clean shirts and dhotis, she in a Punjabi, the loose tunic and trousers, with a little gauze head or breast scarf worn by Mahommedhan girls. All the gardeners' children stood apart; they were Bhramins, the priestly caste, the small girls were exquisite in saris, jessamine flowers in their hair. The dhobi's children were everywhere, some of them dressed only in a charm string and short cotton jacket that left their rice swollen stomachs and private parts bare; the babies wore nothing at all except charm strings, but they were oiled all over. Far over by the door stood the sweeper's son and behind him a smaller boy who, unlike other children, was employed. He had the curious task—for which, touchingly, he would put on his only shirt—of being fetched in to pick up and carry away the bodies of any dead crows that fell into the garden or any casualties among our guinea pigs. No other servant would or could touch a corpse, not even of a pet.

This protocol was not of our seeking; we were often companions of the sweeper's boy—he could fly our kites from the roof better than any of us—but we knew that now, as an untouchable, he must keep apart, just as we knew that the gardener's children must not be given fruit or cakes or sweets; they would not be allowed to eat them because non-Bhramini hands had touched them, non-Bhramini shadows fallen on them, not only non-Bhramini; by Hindu ruling we, as western children, were untouchables as well. It was all part of the intricate web of rules and taboos that govern the whole of Indian social life: children could usually break through it, but not today. This was a public occasion.

'Can't we keep that *darling* little doll? One little basket of cooking pots? One box of chocolates?' But we never could. The answer was always the same and it was the four of us who were required to do the actual giving, acting as reluctant little Lady Bountifuls. My youngest sister Rose was a greedy child and Nan sometimes had literally to prise a drum of Turkish delight or a box of chocolates out of her hand.

We parted first with the fruit and nuts; these were tied swiftly into the corners of saris or dhotis or collected by the dhobi's wife into an old pillow case. (The dhobi's wife always fascinated us because she had elephantiasis. We stared at her gargantuan feet and ankles.) Then each of the children was given an empty cracker box or its lid to hold. These were filled with sweets; the boxes of chocolates were ripped open or given whole to a family. Then the Christmas cakes were allotted and this was done in the unfair way of the world—the largest and best cakes to the richest children, the worst to the neediest, but my mother always kept a collection of inconspicuous pink iced cakes to help fill the maws of the small dhobis. At last came the moment for which everyone was really waiting—the distribution of the toys.

Why was it such a pang to part with these? Why did we like them so much? I suppose because no one else ever gave such things to us. We each had a sensible gift from our father and mother, probably something we had wanted all the year; in the evening we should each get something from the Club Christmas tree, but in this isolated place the dollies brought the only toys we saw from outside the great world, as it were. Some were Indian; miniature brass cooking pots, platters and ladles, or wooden animals, miniature too and painted with spots and red daisies which made them look seductive and all packed in small chip baskets; there were glass bangles in jewel colours which we were not allowed to wear; wonderfully cut paper balls; clay gods and goddesses; and with these were western toys, one for each of us: cheap clockwork cars and trains, wooden animals that clacked and bounced, celluloid toys, dolls with fixed eyes, gummed on clothes, chip straw hats. Here again, the rich had the best; Mahommed Shah's daughter the most splendiferous doll—the dhobi's the collection of celluloids, but immediately after came the crackers as consolation. Crackers were always divided equally.

People say crackers are expensive nonsense. I wish they could have seen those children with them. 'A-aah! A-aah! Aie! Aie!' Murmurs broke out all over the room. The big kohl darkened eyes grew bigger, brown faces broke into smiles; the small brown hands holding the cardboard box trays trembled. Those crackers would be kept long after the things inside had

been taken out; the gaudy fringed papers, the least tinselled star be made a treasure. We liked giving the crackers—by then we had been won over and nothing mattered except that the children should be made as contented as possible; but then the ritual was finished. In a few minutes the last child had salaamed and scurried away; the baskets were picked up empty. Once again everything was gone.

'Look where those children live, and look where you . . .' Nan would scold. We knew quite well where they lived, mostly in a line of brick built rooms behind the cookhouse, one room to a family, one tap to a whole row. The dhobi children lived in the wash court, the grooms in a wicker hut beside the stable, but we did not see anything wrong with this. Indeed, it seemed gloriously simple; no nursery or schoolroom, no coming down to the dining-room for meals, no changing to go into the drawing-room, so few clothes; and to us those little rooms were homelike, with their swept earth floors, clay oven, shelf of brass cooking pots, perhaps a day bed, the straw sleeping mats rolled up, the family possessions in a tin trunk painted with roses, the family umbrella hanging from the rafters. The poorer the house, the prettier, because it did not have such uglinesses as aluminium saucepans, army blankets, china plates, petrol lamps. The children ate off banana leaves with their fingers. At night the soft flicker of a wick floating in an earthenware lamp turned all the walls to gold. 'You are so lucky,' Nan always said. They were lucky too. 'And I don't see,' Rose said obstinately, 'why they should have our toys.'

'You wouldn't want to keep all those?'

'I would.' Rose was firm. She was young enough to say what she thought unabashed, but we could only feel; the fact that we knew we were selfish only made it worse.

'You must not only give, you must love giving.' Perhaps that early training grew into our bones. I do love to give, yet still, somewhere, at the back of my mind is an unsatisfied yearning and I wish that somehow, something that can never happen in far off England, would happen, and I could have one dolly entirely to myself.

I am going to introduce you now to Lord Dunsany.

Lord Dunsany was born Edward Plunkett but he became Lord Dunsany when his father died before he was twenty. He had one brother called Reggie but he never got on well with him for Dunsany was a loving rather boisterous kind of boy, whereas Reggie was the type who kept himself to himself.

Dunsany was educated at a preparatory school, Eton and finally crammers and then joined the Grenadier Guards, with whom he served in the Boer War. In spite of this correct upbringing he seems to have been an extraordinary young man, almost boorish. He danced badly, he spoke his mind without any regard for the person to whom he was speaking, and he was always wrongly dressed. But under all this was what nobody could possibly guess—a real writer struggling to get out.

When you are older you should try and get hold of some of Dunsany's plays, novels, short stories and poetry. All his life he had loved the out-of-doors, particularly wide open spaces. He had a great affinity with gods and goddesses but as well he loved simple story-telling. In this story he re-tells the well-known fable of 'The Tortoise and The Hare'. Notice the splendidly factual way in which he begins—'For a long time there was doubt with acrimony among the beasts'—no arguing. Dunsany is stating a fact. Notice too his superb irony. He really is delightful to read. Think of 'hard shell and hard living' next time someone uses a catch phrase.

The True History of the Hare and the Tortoise

For a long time there was doubt with acrimony among the beasts as to whether the Hare or the Tortoise could run the swifter. Some said the Hare was the swifter of the two because he had such long ears, and others said that the Tortoise was the swifter because anyone whose shell was so hard as that should be able to run too. And lo, the forces of estrangement and disorder perpetually postponed a decisive contest.

But when there was nearly war among the beasts, at last an arrangement was come to and it was decided that the Hare and the Tortoise should run a race of five hundred yards so that all should see who was right.

'Ridiculous nonsense!' said the Hare, and it was all his backers could do to get him to run.

'The contest is most welcome to me,' said the Tortoise. 'I shall not shirk it.'

O, how his backers cheered.

Feeling ran high on the day of the race; the goose rushed at the fox and nearly pecked him. Both sides spoke loudly of the approaching victory up to the very moment of the race.

'I am absolutely confident of success,' said the Tortoise. But the Hare said nothing, he looked bored and cross. Some of his supporters deserted him then and went to the other side, who were loudly cheering the Tortoise's inspiriting words. But many remained with the Hare. 'We shall not be disappointed in him,' they said. 'A beast with such long ears is bound to win.'

'Run hard,' said the supporters of the Tortoise.

And 'run hard' became a kind of catch-phrase which everybody repeated to one another. 'Hard shell and hard living. That's what the country wants. Run hard,' they said. And these words were never uttered but multitudes cheered from their hearts.

Then they were off, and suddenly there was a hush.

The Hare dashed off for about a hundred yards, then he looked round to see where his rival was.

'It is rather absurd,' he said, 'to race with a Tortoise.' And he sat down and scratched himself. 'Run hard! Run hard!' shouted some.

'Let him rest,' shouted others. And 'let him rest' became a catch-phrase too.

And after a while his rival drew near to him.

'There comes that damned Tortoise,' said the Hare, and he got up and ran as hard as he could so that he should not let the Tortoise beat him.

'Those ears will win,' said his friends. 'Those ears will win; and establish upon an incontestable footing the truth of what we have said.' And some of them turned to the backers of the Tortoise and said: 'What about your beast now?'

'Run hard,' they replied. 'Run hard.'

The Hare ran on for nearly three hundred yards, nearly in fact as far as the winning-post, when it suddenly struck him what a fool he looked running races with a Tortoise who was nowhere in sight, and he sat down again and scratched.

'Run hard. Run hard,' said the crowd, and 'Let him rest.'

'Whatever is the use of it?' said the Hare, and this time he stopped for good. Some say he slept.

There was desperate excitement for an hour or two, and then the Tortoise won.

'Run hard. Run hard,' shouted his backers. 'Hard shell and hard living; that's what has done it.' And they asked the Tortoise what his achievement signified and he went and asked the Turtle. And the Turtle said: 'It is a glorious victory for the forces of swiftness.' And then the Tortoise repeated it to his friends. And all the beasts said nothing else for years. And even to this day 'a glorious victory for the forces of swiftness' is a catch-phrase in the house of the snail.

And the reason that this version of the race is not widely known is that very few of those that witnessed it survived the great forest-fire that happened shortly after. It came up over the weald by night with a great wind. The Hare and the Tortoise and a very few of the beasts saw it far off from a high bare hill that was at the edge of the trees, and they hurriedly called a meeting to decide what messenger they should send to warn the beasts in the forest.

They sent the Tortoise.

Grace Darling was born in 1815, which was, as you will remember, the year of Waterloo. She was the seventh of nine children and her father was a lighthouse keeper. When she was growing up those who lived on the Northumberland coast would have told you that the Darlings had always been lighthouse keepers and that William Darling, Grace's father, had been on Longstone Lighthouse on Farne Island from the age of nine, and that he had grown up there and had finally taken over the job of keeper from his father. They would probably have told you, too, that he had taken part in more than sixty rescue operations, saving people from ships that had foundered on the dangerous Harcar Rocks, a mile away from the lighthouse. If they mentioned Grace at all, it would probably be to say that she was a quiet girl, fond of working in the garden and studying the birds that inhabited the island. Some people might have mentioned that Grace Darling was the stay-at-home member of the family for she was not particularly strong.

It sounds as though life at the Longstone Lighthouse was peaceful and perhaps even rather monotonous, but actually Grace and her brothers and sisters were kept pretty well occupied. They were able to clean the lantern and knew how to operate it. They knew lighthouse routine and procedure down to the last rule. And they could all handle the lighthouse boat. This was a Northumbrian coble, twenty-five feet long, five and a half feet broad, fitted for four oars and capable of carrying half a dozen people. Presently the children grew up and went out into the world but Grace stayed at home helping to run the lighthouse.

EDWARD BOYD

The Story of Grace Darling

The incident which has sent Grace Darling's name down to posterity began on 5th September 1838. A small steamer called the *Forfarshire* skippered by Captain John Humble left the port of Hull. There was nothing unusual or dramatic in this. It was, in fact, very ordinary. The *Forfarshire* ran a regular coastal service between Hull and Dundee, carrying cargo and passengers, and this should have been just another trip. True, the weather was threatening, but ships would never sail if they worried about that, and anyway the *Forfarshire* was a fairly new ship and had not long since been inspected and overhauled. So Captain Humble sailed out confidently from the Humber. Including the crew, there were sixty-three people on board as well as a large cargo.

The threatening weather lived up to its threat and grew steadily worse. On the morning following the departure from Hull, one of the ship's boilers began to leak. The safest course would have been for the captain to have turned back but instead he set his crew working at the pumps and carried straight on. The storm increased, and a vicious sea buffeted the *Forfarshire* brutally, straining her still further. The leaking grew worse until, despite the best efforts of the crew, the stokehold and the engine-room were awash. All through the night and during most of the next day, the steamer butted its way forward, making headway only with the greatest difficulty. But as they approached the Firth of Forth, disaster struck. The water in the engine-room put the fires out so that the engines could no longer work.

In those early days of steam, ships still carried sail, so Captain Humble set headsails, hoping, by the use of these, to reach a safe harbour. But by this time the ferocity of the wind was such that all he could do was to run before it. He found himself, therefore, being blown back the way he had come.

Darkness was falling, huge, mountainous seas were crashing

over the ship and the fury of the gale made her practically uncontrollable. In the very early hours of 7th September 1838, the *Forfarshire* was being hurled about the ocean, at the mercy of the elements, not far from Bamborough Castle, off the Northumberland coast. Captain Humble made a last desperate attempt to get his ship into the fairway channel between the mainland and the Farne Islands, but the attempt was a failure and at three o'clock in the morning the pounding seas crashed the unfortunate *Forfarshire* onto the rocks and tore a huge hole in her bows.

One boat managed to get away with nine men in it, but then another great sea took the doomed ship and broke her in two. The after part of the ship was swirled away to destruction, the fore part was firmly wedged against the rocks. Some of the survivors managed to scramble onto these rocks and clung there precariously.

The Darling family had had their own troubles that night for Mr Darling and Grace had had to go out several times to make sure that their coble was safe. It was after returning from one of those check-up trips, about five in the morning, that Grace first discerned the wreck that was piled up on the rocks. It was still too dark to make out details, but later, when the grey stormy morning broke, the survivors, huddled on the rocks, could be seen clearly. Immediately, Grace pleaded to be allowed to take the coble out in an attempt to rescue them. Her father was doubtful. A raging waste of water lay between the lighthouse and the victims of the wreck, and it seemed impossible to cross in the pitifully small coble. But to Grace, the impossibility did not matter. It was necessity that mattered. William Darling listened to her pleading, glanced across at the desperate, forlorn figures on the rocks and hesitated no longer. He called on his wife and with her help, he and Grace pushed the coble off into the wild sea.

For a while, it looked as though the effort they were making was completely in vain. The small boat was flung about as though it weighed nothing at all. The waves broke over it and threatened at any moment to swamp it altogether. Grace and her father had to take a long, roundabout way to the wreck to get what little shelter was available. There were times when it seemed that they had been rowing for hours and when all the heart-bursting muscle-straining effort had resulted in no progress at all. But every now and then, as a huge wave raised the tiny boat aloft, they would catch sight of the helpless people on the rocks. The boat was by then visible to the survivors and some of them were waving. The sight spurred the brave girl and her equally valiant father to mightier efforts yet: and slowly, agonizingly, they drew near to what was left of the *Forfarshire*.

Near the wreck William Darling jumped onto the rocks and began to help the exhausted survivors while Grace managed the boat alone. William Darling found eight men and a woman with her two children, a boy and a girl. The poor little girl had died of exposure and all the others had suffered dreadfully. Four men and a woman were taken on board, that being all that the coble could hold, and while Grace Darling ministered to the poor woman, William Darling and the men rowed the coble to the lighthouse, where the first survivors landed and were given into the efficient care of Mrs Darling.

Grace and her father, together with two of the rescued men, then set off again to complete the rescue. This time, with more people to row, the journey did not take so long, and very soon the coble was on its way back with the remaining survivors. Later, the boat that had been lowered when the *Forfarshire* struck was picked up. Altogether, out of the sixty-three people who had sailed from Hull, only seventeen were left. Had it not been for Grace Darling, there would have been no survivors at all.

As soon as the news of the Longstone Lighthouse rescue appeared, the whole of Britain thrilled with pride. The story of the twenty-two-year-old girl's wonderful heroism was on everyone's lips. Grace Darling received thousands of letters. Some of these were from people who simply wanted to express their admiration and appreciation. Some of them invited her to tour round the country on the stage. All the newspapers were filled with photographs and fulsome flattery. Through it all Grace Darling went on her quiet, attractive way, unaffected by a fuss

that might have turned a weaker head. Wordsworth wrote a poem about her:

'The Maiden gentle, yet, at duty's call
Firm and unflinching as the lighthouse reared
On the Island Rock, her lonely dwelling place.'

It was not a very good poem, but it did express what everyone felt.

Poems and flattery are all right, however, but there were people who felt that something much more practical should be done in recognition of Grace Darling's magnificent courage. The Royal National Lifeboat Institution presented her with its Silver Medal. The Royal Humane Society followed the example and made an award of its Gold Medal. The Government rewarded her with a sum of money, to which was added a considerable sum raised by public subscription. The money was invested for her and her future seemed assured.

Grace did not live long to enjoy the fruits of her heroism and self-sacrifice. Never having been particularly strong and perhaps not really recovered from the tremendous and appalling strain of that wild morning when the *Forfarshire* broke in two on the Harcar Rocks, she had not the strength to throw off a bad illness. The autumn of 1842 was a season of severe and bitter weather, and Grace Darling went down with a chill.

Soon the country was startled by the news that the girl who, four years earlier, had earned the admiration not only of her own country but of the whole world, was now dead. She had died on the 20th October and had been buried at Bamborough while a gale raged round the churchyard. It was a great gale and there were fanciful people who wondered if it was the same gale that she had defied in 1838 and if so whether it had come to pay tribute to her or to claim her at last. But of one thing at least they were certain. No matter how fierce the gales of the future might rage, the example and reputation of Grace Darling would stand proud and unshaken like a rock—or a lighthouse.

Margaret Mahy lives in New Zealand and is a name to watch out for because she is undoubtedly very talented.

It is always sad to see fine old trees cut down, even when, as in this story, they are getting old and not very safe.

When you are reading about Elizabeth's trees do not forget the author is writing about New Zealand. I am afraid there are few places in England where cutting down a few pine trees would mean opening up a glorious view. Lucky New Zealand to have so much space.

MARGARET MAHY

The Trees

Ever since Elizabeth could remember, pine trees had grown along the north fence like a line of giant green soldiers marching down the hill, but today, a bright shining blue and gold day, men were coming to cut them down.

Judith and Colin who were both younger than Elizabeth teased her at breakfast time. They were looking forward to the tree men coming with their axes and saws and they could not understand why Elizabeth was not excited too. The funny thing was Elizabeth could not explain it to them.

'The trees will just *crash* down!' Colin cried. 'Like ninepins knocked over. Don't you even want to hear them crash?'

'I'll hate it,' Elizabeth cried. She felt as if every hair on her head was standing on end with anger.

'Why don't you want to hear it?' asked Judith, looking at Elizabeth with a round solemn face like a freckled owl.

'I just don't!' Elizabeth muttered. She wanted to tell Judith that she loved the tall green pine trees. When she woke up in the morning and looked out of her window they were the first things she saw. Flying above them the magpies would toss and turn in the air making their strange silvery yodelling sound like a musical box gone wrong. When the moon crept over the sky at night Elizabeth saw it through the branches of the pines, and that dark line of trees on the greeny brown hillside was her first sight of home when she came back from town. Because she had climbed them so often she felt she knew every branch and hollow of them by heart. They were all her friends, but the largest tree of all was her favourite because her swing hung from its lowest branch. Elizabeth was growing so tall that she had to tuck her feet right under her when she was on the swing but she still loved swinging. Sometimes she felt the swing might come off and fly away with her to some magic land. It seemed terrible to think that after today she would never again swing high up and see blue sky through a criss-cross of branches and twigs and pine needles. Elizabeth wanted to explain this but somehow she didn't know the right words and even if she did she felt Colin and Judith would not understand them.

'Anyhow,' Colin said guessing her thoughts, 'Daddy says he'll make a new swing for us like one in the park.'

'That won't be the same,' Elizabeth said scornfully. 'It will just be a dead *swing*. The one on the pine tree is alive.'

'You're as mad as mad!' Colin cried. 'Whoever heard of a live swing.'

Daddy looked at them crossly.

'Now you children!' he exclaimed. 'Stop that bickering and sniping. Elizabeth, *I'm* sorry the trees have to be cut down, too—they're seventy years old and were here when grandfather was born. But they've grown too tall, they're just not safe so close to the house any more. They've got to go. I'm not happy about it but there you are!'

'Yes, Daddy,' Elizabeth said. 'I know that,' and she tried to take no more notice of Colin and Judith even when they whispered to each other watching her closely.

'Crash go the pine trees!'

Inside Elizabeth said to herself, 'It won't be like home ever again without the pine trees.'

After breakfast the tree fellers arrived in a truck. The back of the truck was loaded with axes and ropes and tins of lunch. And in the middle of all these things was a winch with wire rope wound round it. There were three tree fellers and they climbed out of the truck and shook hands with Elizabeth's father.

'Hello!' said the tallest man of the three, looking at Judith and Colin. 'Have we got an audience?'

'They've been looking forward to it,' said Daddy. 'Whereas Elizabeth here wants us to keep the trees.' The tall man smiled at Elizabeth. He had white teeth and a brown crinkled face and he was wearing a blue shirt. Elizabeth liked him for a moment then she thought to herself that he was a tree killer and she did not smile back.

'Will you chop the trees down with an axe?' asked Judith.

'No!' said the blue-shirt man. 'We'll use a chain saw.'

'Is that a saw to saw chains through?' Judith asked again but of course she was only five and didn't know much.

'Don't be mad!' said Colin. 'It's a big saw with a motor on it, isn't it? You don't have to push and pull it—the motor drives it and makes it cut, doesn't it?'

'That's right,' said the blue-shirt man. 'I can see you know all about it. Now, let's have a look at these sticks!'

'Sticks!' Colin yelled. 'It's trees you've got to cut down—not sticks.'

'We call the trees sticks,' the blue-shirt man said. 'It stops us from being too frightened of them. It's dangerous cutting down trees you know. They try to fall on us but we're too clever for them. We make them fall where we want them to.'

Elizabeth followed them as they all set off together to look at the trees.

'Sticks!' she thought. 'What a name for lovely green trees.' She watched with a mixed feeling of being interested and sad while the man fastened ropes to the first tree in the line. Then the blue-shirted man started up his chain saw. It roared like a lion until he cut into the tree with it. Then it screamed furiously and the sawdust flew out around the head and shoulders of the blue-shirt man. First he cut a piece out of one side of the tree and then he moved around to the other side where the chain saw screamed and the sawdust flew again. Then he stood back and shouted.

'All right—give her a go.'

The truck engine started up and moved forward by inches. The rope grew tight. Staring at the tree top Elizabeth saw it move as if there was a wind in it—a wind that the other pine trees could not feel. Then it started to fall. Elizabeth held her breath. It fell slowly at first, then faster and faster until it smashed onto the ground with a sound like crashing drums, thunder and tearing sheets. Branches broke. Pine cones flew into the air like startled birds. Judith and Colin screamed with delight.

'Didn't it crash! Gee! Didn't it crash!' yelled Colin.

'I thought it was scratching the sky down,' Judith cried. Elizabeth did not know what to say. It had been exciting to see the tree falling—to see all that great tower of needles, cones, and branches coming down at her (though of course it hadn't landed anywhere near her). Yet now there was a gap in the line of trees like a tooth missing in a smile. She felt sad again.

The chain saw screamed and the truck engine rumbled. Neighbours came to stare. Tree after tree came tumbling down. They lay in a great tangled mass of broken branches and oozing pine gum, smelling of the gum and bruised pine needles. They weren't part of a grand row of trees any more—they were just a mess.

Then it was lunch time. The men got their lunch tins and sat down to eat. Colin and Judith sat down beside them talking, while Elizabeth lurked a little way off, not wanting to join in, but not wanting to miss out on anything. Suddenly the blue-shirt man looked over Colin's head, straight at her.

'You're quiet to-day, lassie,' he said. 'So you're sorry to lose the trees!' Before Elizabeth could reply he went on: 'Think it's sad m'self to see those sticks come down, but some of them are old and tired, really dangerous. And don't you go thinking you're losing out altogether. You're losing the trees, sure, but look at the view. We're not just cutting down trees for your Dad, we're letting in the world.'

Elizabeth looked at the view. Up till now she had been just seeing it as a space where pine trees had been growing. Now she realized she could see right across the valley from her own hill-side to the great greeny-brown hills opposite. In between lay farms and fields and the winding line of the creek with its fringe of poplars and willows. She could see the dark green shapes of the pine trees and firs, and the small white shapes of the sheep with their shadows beside them, short and stumpy because it was mid-day. Elizabeth had a feeling of space and sky she had never had before. Deep down inside her she knew that she would come to love this even more than she had loved her pine trees.

She looked at the blue-shirt man and smiled uncertainly.

'It *is* lovely,' she said, and she really meant it.

During the afternoon when the rest of the trees came down Elizabeth looked at the widening space they left with a different feeling. She saw still more of the hills and the widening wandering creek come out from behind the pine trees. The new view was like a butterfly struggling out of its chrysalis—something gained not lost.

At last there was only the swing tree left. Elizabeth did not want to watch it fall. She went inside but all the time her ears were listening for the crash. It did not come. Instead she heard the truck starting up and going away again. When she looked out of the window she saw her new wide view and at the very end of it a single green soldier stood on guard—the swing tree.

Out ran Elizabeth into the kitchen where Colin and Judith were eating bread and jam. When Colin saw her he said:

'Anyhow, they didn't cut down your old swing tree so there. It's still a strong tree and not anywhere near the house so the blue-shirt man asked Daddy and Daddy said to leave it.'

'It was the biggest tree of all,' said Judith, but Elizabeth scarcely heard her. She ran out into the yard. It was not easy to get to the swing tree now, for the back of the yard was filled with the fallen pines, but Elizabeth wove her way over and under the grey trunks and branches. At last she stood under the old tree. She touched the swing dangling from it. She looked up at the sky through its branches and felt its rough bark under her hand.

'Hello!' she said softly, 'are you still here?' Then she got on the swing and worked her way up high sweeping backwards and forwards in a long swooping line. Above her the pine tree rustled and whispered as if it was talking to her. As she swung there, she suddenly thought of the blue-shirt man and wished she had said thank you.

Stevie Smith was an original. She was one of those people who, without doing anything conspicuous, stood out in a crowded room.

When people—especially young people—liked hearing poets read out loud their own poetry, Stevie Smith was in great demand for her poetry was lovely and she knew how it should sound when read. Then, suddenly she died and this world is the poorer without her.

Here is one of her poems. I hope you will love it as much as I do.

The Heavenly City

I sigh for the heavenly country,
Where the heavenly people pass,
And the sea is as quiet as a mirror
Of beautiful, beautiful glass.

I walk in the heavenly field,
With lilies and poppies bright,
I am dressed in a heavenly coat
Of polished white.

When I walk in the heavenly parkland
My feet on the pastures are bare,
Tall waves the grass, but no harmful
Creature is there.

At night I fly over the housetops,
And stand on the bright moony beams;
Gold are all heaven's rivers,
And silver her streams.

Stevie Smith

I have always loved peacocks. When I was a child and went to stay with Granny and Grandfather, who were my father's mother and father, they kept peacocks. Staying away is usually exciting just because everything is different from home, but at Granny and Grandfather's the most different thing was the peacocks. Grandfather did not keep many peacocks—four I think, two cocks and two hens. The cocks strutted around as proud as proud displaying their gorgeous feathers, the hens, especially on wet days, making the most dismal cries. We never envied Grandfather his peacocks because at home we only had a lawn not much bigger than a sheet so we could not have kept a peacock even if we had been given one. But knowing four peacocks has left me fond of them for always.

Imagine how pleased I was then, when searching for a fairy story for this book, to find one full of peacocks. And what peacocks! You read this story and you will see what I mean.

SARAH STAFFORD SMITH

The Moonlight Bird

In the forests of northern India, thousands of years ago, there lived a magnificent peacock, the finest in the land. Now the King of that region and all his courtiers hunted in those forests and, although they preferred to capture or kill some great beast such as an elephant or a leopard, they were not above snaring an occasional peacock. If its plumage was especially gorgeous, they brought it back alive to beautify the King's garden. Everybody who was anybody had peacocks in their gardens in those days, just as they are inclined to do in many parts of the world today. If the bird was less magnificent, it might be shot to supply a tasty dish for the King's table.

One day, the King himself caught sight of this finest of all peacocks spreading his wonderful plumage in a sunlit clearing and realized that here was the most brilliant and beautiful bird he had ever seen. The peacock's mate stood near by, looking very dull and drab beside her elegant husband. The King sent huntsmen to capture them both and they were taken to live in the palace gardens. The King gave the peacock a name. 'He shall be called Org!' he said.

Now it happened that this King was a harsh and cruel man and there was no justice in the kingdom in his reign. His dungeons were filled with prisoners who had never been brought to trial or allowed to speak in their own defence. His daughter, whose beauty was a legend in the land, was kept under guard in her magnificent apartments and never permitted to leave the palace. Many princes begged for her hand in marriage, but the King sent them all away. He knew that a marriage to a prince would mean an alliance with another kingdom and an alliance would make him less important. Besides, he did not believe that even the finest prince was good enough for his daughter. She was his most treasured possession and he guarded her with the utmost jealousy. Even Prince Ali from the Eastern Kingdom, who was as handsome as the Princess was beautiful and as wealthy as the King himself, even he was sent away, but not before the Princess, watching from among the flowering trees on her marble terrace, had seen him walking in the garden and fallen in love with him on the spot. But her love was hopeless, for she was afraid of her cruel father and so, of course, were all the courtiers and so, indeed, was everybody in the land, except for one man. This was Kol, the Court Magician, and of him even the King himself was more than a little afraid. Kol was neither harsh nor cruel and he was immensely wise. He saw that the people were too terrified of the King to rise in rebellion and he knew that none of the surrounding kingdoms had ever won a battle against him. As Court Magician, Kol could not use his magic directly against the King, so he set to work to think of some other way of saving the land from this man's tyranny.

'Armies cannot prevail against him,' said Kol to himself. 'The whole nation is under his evil sway. I will make a magic so that he is brought low, not by me, but by some very small thing.'

One night, as Kol was walking in the Palace gardens by the light of a full moon, he came upon Org, the peacock, standing on a smooth lawn under a sumac tree. As Kol approached, Org spread the wonderful coverts of his tail and uttered a cry which Kol at once understood. Looking up into the sumac tree, he saw the mate sitting on her nest. A moment later, she rose up and perched on a nearby branch and Kol looked into the nest and saw, not four or five eggs, as he had expected, but one solitary egg.

'Here,' he said to himself, 'is the one small thing by which the King shall be brought low.'

And he pronounced a spell upon the egg and touched it with his magic ring and went away and the mother bird settled once more upon the nest.

When the chick was hatched, he looked exactly like any other infant peacock, but his parents were as proud of him as if the sun shone out of his fluffy head. Parents are like that. Time went by and the chick became a fully-grown bird and the coverts of his tail were longer and more brilliant than those of Org himself. The King was intensely proud of his new peacock and issued a command that all his courtiers, when they met the bird in the gardens, should greet him with a humble bow. The courtiers grumbled among themselves but did not dare to disobey the order. The King gave a name to his new peacock. 'He shall be called Van!' he said.

So Van, the son of Org, strutted about the garden, enjoying the sunshine and the shade, the water in the marble basins, the brilliant flowers with their exquisite perfumes and the trees, which reminded him of something he had never known. If this sounds absurd, it must be remembered that the peacock is a forest bird, so Van had an instinct for trees and longed for the forest without understanding why.

He enjoyed, too, the humble bows of the courtiers. Everyone bowed to him except the King himself and a certain man with a long beard, who walked in the garden on moonlight nights. As Van strutted among the courtiers, he listened to their talk and, little by little, he learned the speech of men, for Kol, by his magic, had endowed him with some of his own wisdom. Van, however, used his knowledge only for listening, never for speech until, one night, he saw the man with the long beard who never bowed to him, walking in the moonlight.

'Why do you never bow to me?' asked Van. 'I am Van, the son of Org, and this garden belongs to me!'

Kol was not in the least surprised to find that the peacock could speak and he smiled in his beard and said:

'You are Van, the son of Org, and you are the wisest creature in this garden!'

The bird spread his fan of feathers and stretched his neck to its full length.

'But,' went on Kol, 'your wisdom in only a measure of my own, which I bestowed upon you while you were yet in the shell. I can as easily take it back and you will be foolish like the rest.'

'Why did you give me this wisdom?' asked Van. 'I have learned from the courtiers that nothing is given freely in this kingdom. Nothing is given without hope of return. What do you want of me in return for this wisdom?'

And Kol replied, 'Proud you will always be, since you are the son of Org. Vain you will always be after the manner of your kind. But there is one in this kingdom who is not only proud and vain, but also cruel, tyrannical and unjust, jealous and evil beyond imagining. I may not use my magic directly against him, but it is your destiny to bring him to naught.'

'You mean, without a doubt, the King!' said Van.

'I mean the King,' said Kol.

'I have heard that he has all the faults you mention,' said Van. 'The courtiers never tire of whispering about them among themselves, but I am Van, the son of Org, and, by the King's command I live in this garden and this garden belongs to me!'

'Nevertheless,' said Kol, 'the King is evil and if you bring him low, the whole kingdom will praise you and your fame will spread far beyond this garden to the utmost confines of the land!'

Then Van puffed himself up until the crest on his head trembled with importance.

'Leave it to me!' he said and settled down in the sumac tree to think.

He thought for one hour, twenty-nine and a half minutes and then, suddenly, he knew what he must do and began to make his plans. He waited until the night before the next new moon, when he knew he would meet Kol, walking in the garden.

'I am ready,' said Van, 'to do as you require, but I shall need your help in two small particulars.'

'And what are they?' asked Kol, smiling in his beard to think that the King's downfall was drawing near at last.

'First you must put it into the mind of Prince Ali of the Eastern Kingdom that he must be at the gates of this garden tomorrow night at midnight, on his horse which is caparisoned in gold and runs like the wind, and he must bring a second horse, as fast as his own and caparisoned in silver. That is my first request and my second is that you should arrange for the gates to be unlocked and all the guards asleep when the Prince arrives.'

'It shall be done,' said Kol.

The following day, at sunset, Prince Ali called his servant to bring his horse caparisoned in gold and another, caparisoned in silver, and have them ready in the courtyard. The servant stared at his master in astonishment.

'Your Highness,' he said, 'it will soon be dark. Will you ride by moonlight?'

'Yes,' replied the Prince, 'I must, and alone. Do as I bid you!' But he looked quite as bewildered as his servant had done.

Meanwhile Van waited for nightfall and took up his position below the Princess's marble terrace. Now, the Princess had the habit of sending her maidens away each evening and walking alone on the terrace for an hour in the cool of the day. Just at that moment of moonrise, Van flew up and perched on the balustrade and spread out his covert feathers in a magnificent fan. It was not the first time he had done this and the Princess, while she admired the display, was not in the least surprised. Then he spoke and the Princess started back, scarcely able to believe her ears.

'Beautiful Princess!' said the bird, 'trust me! For I am Van, the son of Org, and this garden belongs to me! I can give you happiness and freedom, but first you must answer one question and then you must do as I say. Do you love Prince Ali of the Eastern Kingdom?'

'I do!' replied the Princess. 'But how is it that you, a bird, can speak with the speech of men?'

'That you shall learn, all in good time. Now, do as I say! At midnight Prince Ali will be at the Palace gates on a horse caparisoned in gold, with a horse caparisoned in silver beside him. This second horse is for you and you must be ready to leave at once and ride with him to the Eastern Kingdom. Tell no one of this and take nothing with you except your jewels.'

Then the Princess trembled with joy and fear.

'But the gates are guarded,' she said, 'and if my father learns of this, he will imprison me and slay the Prince!'

'The gates will be open,' said Van, 'and the guards will be asleep.'

'I dare not!' said the Princess, shrinking back. 'I dare not!'

'You must!' said Van. 'I shall return two hours before midnight and again a third time. If, on my third visit, you dare not obey me, it will be too late!'

Then he flew to the ground and the Princess wept with fear and joy, but she told her maidens that she wished to be alone that night and they went away, knowing that the doors were guarded and the Princess could not escape. Two hours before midnight the bird appeared again and spoke as he had spoken before and again the Princess replied, 'I dare not!' But she had put on her most beautiful sari and placed her jewel-casket beside her on the terrace.

Just before midnight, Van reappeared. Before he so much as opened his beak, the Princess said, 'I am ready!'

'Follow me!' said Van and, fluttering to the terrace pavement, he led the way, hopping from step to step, down the marble staircase, past the sleeping guards, and strutted through the silent garden to the Palace gates. These stood wide open and there was Prince Ali, waiting with the two horses. He dismounted and, kneeling swiftly on one knee, kissed the hand of the Princess, then helped her to mount the beautiful horse with the silver trappings.

'Farewell, marvellous bird!' cried the Princess. 'How can I ever thank you?'

So the Prince and the Princess rode away to the Eastern Kingdom and Van went back through the garden, while the gates closed silently and the guards woke up and did not even know that they had been asleep. Under the sumac tree Van met Kol.

'So far, so good!' he said.

The next morning the whole Palace was in an uproar when it was found that the Princess had disappeared. All her maidens were thrown into prison and all her guards were condemned to death. The King ordered a search to be made in every corner of the land. He summoned Kol and commanded him to use his magic to find the Princess.

'Alas, Majesty!' said Kol, 'I cannot help you, but there is one in your court who, it may be, could lead you to your daughter.'

'Bring him before me!' commanded the King. 'If he will lead me to my daughter, I swear by my crown that I will follow him anywhere! Anywhere!'

So Kol went out into the garden and brought in Van, who stood before the King, his beautiful feathers spread in a fan, and bowed three times. The King looked at the bird, then at Kol and roared in fury:

'Why do you mock me? This is only a peacock!'

Then Van bowed again and said:

'May it please Your Majesty, I am Van the son of Org, and at Your Majesty's command I live in those gardens and they belong to me!'

The King almost fell off his throne with surprise.

'This is your doing, Kol!' he shouted. 'Why have I not been told that this bird could speak?'

'Majesty,' replied Kol, 'it was not I who taught this bird to speak. Let it suffice that he *can* speak and that he can lead you to your daughter!'

'Where *is* my daughter?' roared the King.

'Follow me, Majesty,' said Van, 'and I will show you.'

The King rose up, and, taking off his crown, set it upon a cushion that his Chamberlain held before him and, calling for his horse, he wrapped his mantle about him and prepared to follow Van.

'Majesty,' said the bird, 'you must follow me on foot or you will never find your daughter.'

Then the King flew into a rage and sent for the Captain of the Guard and shouted:

'Prepare the army to follow me! Whoever has stolen the Princess shall pay dearly for it!'

'Majesty,' said Van, 'none may follow you or you will never find your daughter.'

The King was speechless with fury but, having sworn by his crown to follow whoever should lead him to his daughter, he was bound to keep his word or lose his crown. So he dismissed the Captain of the Guard and set out on foot after Van, seething with anger. The outer gates opened of their own accord as they approached and the trembling guards saluted as if it were the most usual thing in the world to see their King, preceded by a peacock, leaving the Palace on foot and alone.

The King was relieved to find that, instead of leading him towards the city, where his subjects could witness his humiliation, Van took the road to the forest, but soon the King was struggling through the undergrowth, while Van fluttered or hopped before him with the greatest of ease. Before long, the King's mantle was torn by brambles and his hands and face were scratched by thorns. He was a sorry sight, but worse was to come. As they emerged from the forest, the King found himself knee-deep in a quagmire. Here and there a boulder or a stunted tree rose from the swampy ground and Van flew from one to the other as if he were enjoying the journey, as, indeed, he was.

The wretched King floundered along behind him, uttering curses and planning his revenge on those who had robbed him of his daughter. At last the quagmire gave way to solid ground, but by now night had fallen and the King was so weary that he called to Van to stop and let him rest. But Van did not even turn his head and the King was obiiged to struggle on. All night they travelled and, just as the sun was rising, Van perched on a rock and the King sank to the ground, utterly exhausted.

'Majesty,' said the bird, 'we are near to the place where your daughter is. Take your girdle and blindfold your eyes, for you may not see the gate. Then take hold of the coverts of my tail and I will lead you to a place from which you may see the Princess without being seen by her.'

The King, by now, was so weary and dispirited that he had not the strength to be angry and, knowing that the journey would

soon be over and his daughter found, he did as the bird commanded. So they approached the gates and were greeted by loud laughter and mocking cries. The King could not know that the gates were those of his own Palace, and the laughter that of his own guards, for Van had led him in a circle back to his starting-point. Neither could he know that Kol had brought the Princess back to the Palace, with Ali, now her husband. They had ridden through the night on the horses caparisoned in gold and silver and very splendid they had looked in their wedding robes as they entered the Palace that morning, to the great rejoicing of all the people.

Whether or not the guards at the gates recognized in this ragged, blindfold fellow, holding onto a peacock's tail the King who had set forth in his splendid mantle, albeit on foot, the day before, we shall never know, but if they did, their laughter must have been all the louder for that. Van led the King up a staircase to a gallery from which he could look down through a lattice into the throne-room itself.

'Majesty,' said the bird, 'you may uncover your eyes.'

So the King tore off the girdle and, looking down, saw the Princess seated upon a jewelled throne, *his* throne, and, beside her, Prince Ali of the Eastern Kingdom. The room was filled with courtiers, all cheering and shouting, 'Long live the Queen! Long live Prince Ali!'

The King turned and rushed down the stairs yelling, 'I am the King! I am the King! Do you not know me?'

Before the Princess could possibly have heard the shouts of the King, he was seized by guards, hustled away and thrown into the deepest dungeon and whether or not the guards recognized their King in this seeming madman, we shall never know, but if they did, they were all the happier for that.

As for Van, son of Org, the Princess knew that it was to him she owed her happiness and the liberation of the land and, as Kol had foretold, his fame spread far and wide and he stood beside the throne on every important occasion and the courtiers bowed to him, no longer because they had been ordered to do so, but out of sheer gratitude. The Princess believed that Van had led her father away to a secret destination and no one told her otherwise. She and Prince Ali declared their two kingdoms to be one and ruled them both in justice and prosperity.

For a year and a day the King lay in prison, bemoaning his fate and begging his guards to let him see the Queen. Then, one morning, came the news that a son had been born to the royal couple and the Queen, to celebrate the event, had ordered the release of all prisoners, though few now remained in the Palace dungeons. So the old King was led up into the light of day, conducted outside the Palace gates and left there, free at last.

He wandered about the city and saw that the people were busy and cheerful and heard, on every side, the praises of King Ali and his beautiful Queen. The light bewildered him after a year in semi-darkness, but he sat down on a bench in one of the city squares to enjoy the sunshine. A poor man, though far less ragged than himself, came and sat down beside him and, opening a leather pouch, brought out bread, cheese and fruit. He turned to the old King.

'You look hungry, my friend,' he said. 'You must be a newcomer to this city. Here, take some of my bread and cheese and we will share a meal together.'

The King accepted the food gladly, for he had felt half-starved in prison, though he had received far more than he had ever allowed his own prisoners. The man watched him eating ravenously and said:

'There is no need to go hungry in this kingdom any more. The new King, Ali, and his beautiful Queen have given work to the strong and bread to the needy. Now, in the old King's days there were many who died of hunger at his very gates, but he cared nothing for them! What a cruel, evil man he was! What a mercy for us all that he is gone!'

'What became of him?' asked the old king, trembling.

'Some say that Van, the son of Org, the Royal Peacock, who speaks with the voice of a man, led him into a quagmire, where he sank. Others whisper that he was thrown into his own dungeons and died there. A few fear he may return, but if he does,

King Ali will be more than a match for him and, in any case, he would find none to fight for him!'

When the meal was over, the man went away and the old king fell asleep in the sun. When he awoke it was night and the moon was already high and there, in the moonlight, standing silently before him were Kol, the magician and Van, the son of Org.

'Are you the King?' asked Kol.

'No! No!' cried the old man. 'I *was* the King, but now I want nothing but a sight of my daughter and a chance to ask her forgiveness.'

'You have answered well,' said Van. 'Follow us!'

So they led him back to the Palace gates, which opened for them of their own accord, and took him to a small apartment, where he was bathed, shaved and dressed in decent apparel. There he rested and early the next morning he was brought before the Queen, a tired old man, worn out by hardships and misery. The Queen wept with pity for him, but Kol said:

'Do not weep, Majesty! It was the price of freedom for this realm and your father has lived to see a happy kingdom and to repent of the evil of his ways.'

So the Queen and her father met again with tears and the old man made his peace with Ali and called down blessings on the baby Prince. Then he went back to the small apartment, lay down upon the bed and died.

That night, as Kol was walking in the moonlight, he came upon Van, the son of Org, standing beneath the sumac tree.

'Your work is done,' said Kol. 'Now you may go to the forest and live as your father, Org, lived before you. No hunter shall snare you and your mate will give you many sons.'

And Van, the son of Org, opened his beak to reply and could not utter a single word, only the cry that peacocks give when they are well content.

I do like now and again to feel my hair stand on end and the cold creep down my spine. Times when I whisper, 'From ghoulies and ghosties and long-leggety beasties and things that go bump in the night, Good Lord deliver us.'

This next story is a spine chiller. It is about witches and Mollie Hunter, who wrote it, is just the right writer for such a creepy affair.

Witches today are not of course what they were. I think they began to lose their powers with the coming of gaslight and they almost entirely lost them when electricity arrived. It is hard to believe in spells in rooms flooded with electric light and blaring with noise from the television set.

All the same anyone is a fool who forgets the powers of evil. We may never meet a witch and laugh at the thought of effigies, but we should always keep an eye out for things which go bump in the night.

MOLLIE HUNTER

The Midsummer Charm

Fifty yards away from his planned confrontation with the witch called Black Sarah, Robert Armett rode his horse into the shelter of a birchwood copse. Half a mile behind him was Colstoun Hall where his father, the Laird of Colstoun, lay dying of the spell Black Sarah had cast on him. Ahead was the squat, thatched house occupied by the witch and her daughter. Gently drawing rein, Robert considered how best he could manage to surprise these two with his presence.

There was still light persisting, late in the day as it was by then; that curiously unshadowed light which lingers long after sundown in a Scottish summer. As so often happens too, in these long summer evenings of northern parts, the air was so quiet that even the most distant sounds—the bleating of a half-grown lamb from some far hillside, a voice calling suddenly from a homestead miles away—were carried with an eerie perfection of clarity.

Robert Armett was seventeen years old in that summer of 1692, a well-built but not unimaginative seventeen; and as always, when he was abroad late on such an evening, he was aware of the influence of these strangely shadowless hours that seemed to belong neither to night nor to day. As always, he was aware of their stillness, and the unreal perfection of far sounds that helped to give them their dreamlike quality.

Now, with the errand on which he was bent, he could also feel something almost sinister in their quiet brooding, and he was irritated to find himself trembling a little as he dismounted to tie his horse to one of the birch trees. He would need to keep a tight rein on fancy, he warned himself. It was all very well for his mother and sister to credit this Black Sarah with supernatural powers, but he was an educated man and should be above such foolishness.

With deliberate calm, he slid his musket from its saddle-holster, charged it, and tamped down the charge. Then carefully he loaded it with the silver bullet his mother had provided.

'If you do not believe it takes a silver bullet to kill a witch, then Black Sarah certainly does,' Lady Colstoun assured him. Which was sound enough reasoning, Robert admitted, and at least the silver bullet would be as effective as an ordinary one.

Cautiously he left the shelter of the trees and began a circling movement to avoid the line of vision from the one small, shuttered window of the witch's house. There was smoke coming from its single chimney, which he hoped was proof that Black Sarah was at home. But in any case, he had already decided, he must act as if that were so.

His circling movement brought him up eventually on the doorstep of the house, and pausing there, he eased back the hammer of his musket. The door in front of him was the usual one for a house of this sort; nothing more than an ox-hide stretched tightly over a light wooden frame. It would be easy to burst through it and take the witch by surprise. Also, his weapon was a modern one with the new flint-lock action, which meant he could depend on it not to misfire!

Robert braced himself for a thrust against the door, then threw all his weight behind one quick plunge of a muscular shoulder. The door gave immediately under the impact, and he found himself blundering forward into the room behind the small shuttered window. A shaft of the pale evening light followed him, but beyond this there was only the flame of a fire leaping on the hearth to show him the room's interior. He blinked rapidly, adjusting his focus, and saw the witch standing by the fire staring in astonishment at him.

Another face stared at him, the face of the witch's daughter crouching by the hearth, but his gaze swept over this crouching figure to rest on the witch's right hand, still frozen in the gesture he had interrupted; and with a shout of anger he jerked his musket up to the firing position.

'Take that thing away from the fire! Take it away, d'ye hear? Or I will shoot—and 'tis a silver bullet I have ready for you!'

The witch glanced down at the fire-tongs in her right hand, and at the little wax figure gripped between the points of the tongs.

'And kill your father?'

Her voice high and scornful, she threw the question at him, then deliberately turned to centre the points of the tongs above the leaping flames on the hearth.

'I can open my hand quicker than you can pull the trigger of that musket,' she went on in the same scornful voice, 'and the instant I do that, this figure will fall into the fire, and your father will die. But in the meantime, my bold young master'—her voice cracked suddenly with hoarse laughter—'in the meantime, see how the wax softens and sweats! See how *he* melts and sweats with the fever I have cast on him!'

'For God's sake——!'

With a cold prickling up his spine, Robert eyed the softening wax. A picture of his father moaning and tossing in the grip of his fever thrust itself into his mind, and all reasoning power vanished in a surge of blind, primitive fear. Hastily he brought the butt of the musket thudding to the earthen floor of the room and blurted:

'There is no threat to you now—look! Take the image away from the fire now, I beg you!'

Slowly the witch turned away from the fire, letting the hand holding the tongs drop to her side as she turned. She faced Robert, insolently letting her dark eyes rake him up and down, and he flushed angrily under the look yet still felt fear underlying the anger.

And that was all wrong, he told himself resentfully. She was only an ignorant peasant, after all, and he was the Laird's son. It was she who should be afraid of him—and yet. . . . There was a force of personality about her, an evil force he had not counted on when he set off so hastily for this confrontation.

'So Lady Colstoun has summoned her tall young son home from the university, has she?' Mockingly Black Sarah's voice broke into his thoughts. 'To deal with the witch, eh? And what has she told you about me, Master Armett?'

'Nothing more than I can see with my own eyes,' he retorted. 'You have made an image of my father and stuck it full of pins to cast pain on him. And now you are holding the beastly thing over your fire, so that his flesh will melt with the heat of fever until he dies.'

The witch stared thoughtfully at him. 'And how did Lady Colstoun know all that?'

'She guessed it from the nature of my father's illness,' Robert told her sullenly. 'And she knew you wanted revenge on him.'

'And I will have that revenge!' Her voice suddenly vicious, Black Sarah shot the words at him. 'It was your father who had me arrested for witchcraft two months ago, Master Robert Armett. It was . . .'

'But the court acquitted you!' Robert interrupted. 'You suffered no harm!'

'That was no thanks to the Laird,' Black Sarah retorted. 'The court freed me for lack of evidence, Master Armett, and now——'

'Now I have that evidence!' Robert interrupted her again, and with assurance flowing back into him, he pointed to the wax image. '*That* will be enough to convict you this time!'

Black Sarah laughed. 'Take it!' she invited, and held the fire-tongs out at arm's length in front of her. 'Take it, and hold it as evidence, Master Armett. But remember the law's delays. Think of the power that is in this image. And be warned that your father will die of the spell it has cast on him long before *I* can be brought to book.'

Robert stared at the grotesque little figure gripped between the points of the tongs. An academic discussion on the existence of witchcraft was one thing, he thought uneasily, but here was none of the sensibly-reassuring atmosphere of the University common-room. Indeed, there was something uncanny here, something genuinely evil. Had he any right to risk his father's life by denying the truth of that? Or by doubting that the image had the power the witch claimed for it?

'I could make you destroy it,' he said hoarsely. 'That would save my father.'

'True,' she agreed. 'But I could make another one, Master Armett. And moreover, what evidence would you have against me if the image was destroyed? It would be your word against mine, in that case, and the law of the land requires at least two witnesses to any criminal act.'

She was clever, Robert admitted to himself; and she could not be so ignorant after all if she knew so much of the law! Rage swept him again suddenly. With an effort he controlled it, and answered as levelly as he could.

'So we are at stalemate. I admit that. But mark me well now, for I will not repeat what I have to say finally to you. You have said plainly that you are bewitching my father; and if he dies of the illness you claim to have cast on him, I will kill *you*!'

The insolence faded from Black Sarah's face. Her gaze became intent, as if she were carefully measuring the strength of purpose behind his words, and when she spoke again her own words were measured and thoughtful.

'I believe you would, Robert Armett. I believe you just would!'

In the silent moment that followed this reply, Robert felt a touch on his ankle; and dropping his gaze from hers, he looked quickly down for the source of the touch. Involuntarily then, he took a step backwards, for the young woman who had been crouching at Black Sarah's feet had edged nearer to him, and he realized it was she who had touched him. One of her hands was still half-raised in the gesture of reaching out to his ankle. Her face was upturned to look at him, and she was smiling in such a sly and strangely malicious way that, with a shiver of distaste, he stepped even farther back from her. Black Sarah laughed, and said with mock reproof in her voice:

'Never shrink from Leezie, Master Armett. She will not like that—will you, Leezie?'

'If you believe me,' Robert pressed on, ignoring the interruption, 'then you know what to do now. Give me the image so that I can destroy it. And be warned for the future, that if you try any more such tricks you will certainly die.'

The girl Leezie crept forward to caress his ankle again, but this time he ignored her and held his ground as he waited for Black Sarah to reply. She took her time about this, but said eventually:

'And supposing I told you, Master Armett, that I want my revenge against your father so badly that I am willing to die for it?'

'That would be stalemate again,' Robert acknowledged, 'but at least you would no longer be alive to trouble the rest of my family.'

Black Sarah said nothing to this, and in a hard voice he told her: 'Take your choice, witch. Kill my father, now or later, and you will die either now or later. Or give me the image and live.'

Still Black Sarah made no reply. She was staring at Leezie, watching her edge nearer and nearer to Robert until she could lay her cheek against his stockinged leg, and realizing how close the girl had now managed to come to him, Robert looked down also. Leezie raised her smiling face to him, and he looked away from her, rigid with distaste yet not knowing how to escape without embarrassment from her grip.

'Aye, you would kill me,' Black Sarah observed maliciously, 'yet still you are too much the gentleman to push my poor Leezie from you!'

'She has done me no harm,' Robert countered stiffly.

'And she likes you. See how she lays her cheek against you!'

Involuntarily Robert obeyed Black Sarah's urging and looked down at Leezie again. It was the first time he had ever really looked close at her, he realized, and for all she seemed lithe and shapely enough he could see now that she was nearly middle-aged—twenty-five, he guessed, if she was a day.

There was something oddly repellent in her features, too—a malevolence in her sly smile, a weirdly animal look about her eyes. They were slitted like those of a cat, he thought—indeed, that was what she looked like—a sly, cruel, intelligent cat! Clearly it was not simply her mother's evil reputation which had thus far frightened all the village lads out of marriage with her, for what man in his senses would wed with such an uncanny-looking creature! And was she deaf and dumb too, that she had seemingly taken no interest in all that had gone on between the witch and himself?

'Tell her to get away from me,' he said sharply to Black Sarah, 'and either destroy the image *now*, or die for it!'

With a firm gesture he made to swing his musket up again, but it was still only half way to his shoulder when Leezie proved she was neither deaf nor dumb. Uncoiling from her crouch and all in the one fluid movement, she seized her mother by the shoulder and hissed:

'Bargain with him. For me, d'ye hear? Bargain with him!'

Black Sarah stared into her daughter's eyes. 'Calm yourself, my lovely,' she said softly. 'I read your thoughts, and my Leezie shall have her Midsummer charm.'

The smile came back to Leezie's face. Black Sarah smiled also—like a mother tiger grinning, Robert thought uneasily—then she turned to confront the long barrel of his musket.

'Hark to me, Master Armett,' she said briskly, 'for here is a bargain that will break the stalemate between us. I will remove the spell I have cast on your father if you will freely do as I say in another matter.'

Slowly Robert lowered the pointing barrel, and harshly he asked, 'What matter?'

Black Sarah hedged with her reply, building on the advantage she had gained with the speed of her opening move. 'Something that can only be managed to its best effect at this particular time of the year. Tomorrow night, to be exact; on Midsummer's Eve.'

'Go on,' Robert commanded. He was staring in open curiosity at her now, but she was still not to be rushed. 'I want to lay a spell then, Master Armett,' she told him. 'A very different kind from the one I laid on your father.'

'And you think *I* will help you? You must be crazy, woman!'

'You will help me,' Black Sarah assured him, '—that is, if you want to save your father. And see, here is an earnest of my good intentions in the bargain!'

With quick, deft movements, she began to extract the pins from the waxen image in her hands, and glanced up with a look of sly triumph as the last one was removed.

'The Laird is free of pain now,' she told Robert. 'You will find that so on your return home tonight. And in the moment you give me what I need to make this other spell, the image itself will be destroyed and he will recover his health again. So, what d'ye say, Master Armett?'

'Give you what you need?' With ever-deepening suspicion taking over from his curiosity, Robert stared from the witch to her daughter. Black Sarah's face was tense, but serious. Leezie was tense in a different way. Her cheeks were puffed out and scarlet, and she had a fist crammed to her mouth to suppress the scream of laughter that threatened to break out. There was a glitter of almost manic glee in the eyes peering out above this fist, and all Robert's suspicions sharpened to focus on the message these signs conveyed.

'What—sort of a spell is this?' With an effort switching his gaze from Leezie, he spoke to Black Sarah again. 'And on whom is it to be cast?'

Black Sarah's eyes bored into his, so that even if he had willed it, he could not have looked away from her then. In low, harsh tones she answered him.

'It will be a love-charm, Master Armett; a love-charm for my Leezie. And the young man it will be cast upon is yourself.'

The laughter Leezie had been stifling broke out suddenly in a wailing shriek, and dazedly through the noise of it, Robert heard Black Sarah ask:

'Will you take my bargain, Master Armett?'

'Let me think, let me think. ...' Desperately his mind raced about, examining every aspect of her proposal, but with each moment that passed he was more aware of the diabolical cunning behind it. The witch was after more than a lover for her daughter, he realized. It was a husband she wanted, and if she got the Laird of Colstoun's son for a husband, the Laird himself could never again pursue her for witchcraft. Not without bringing shame on his own family!

With sweat breaking out on him now, Robert tried to focus his thoughts on the main issue. If he did not take the witch's bargain, she would instantly cast that image into the fire, and his father might die—but he dared not put that 'might' to the test! On the other hand, if he did take her bargain, he would at least buy himself time to think of some way of finally nailing her crimes—perhaps even by springing a confession out of her before witnesses! That would be evidence that would stand up in any court of law, and it was the way his father had always advocated. If he could do that, and make sure that the image was destroyed in the meantime. ...'

'Well, Master Armett?' Black Sarah was becoming impatient. 'Have you an answer for me?'

Robert nodded. Through dry lips he said, 'I'll take your bargain, witch. Say what you want of me.'

Triumph gleamed in Black Sarah's eyes. 'I want,' she said, 'that you should bring me a fair-sized piece of whatever garment you intend shall be worn nearest your heart at twelve o'clock tomorrow night—that is, at midnight on Midsummer's Eve. When you give me that, Master Armett, I shall destroy the image before your eyes. And then'— her eyes slid sideways to Leezie —'and then I shall cast a spell on this piece of your body-linen, and at nine o'clock on the following night this spell will draw you to the churchyard of Colstoun Parish Church, to tryst there with Leezie. Do you understand me, Master Armett?'

Robert nodded, not trusting himself to speak, and Black Sarah added, 'Whatever you are doing then, wherever you may be, this spell will draw you to Leezie's side, and you will never want to leave it again. Do you understand *that*, Master Armett?'

Once again Robert nodded, and as if the action had triggered off the sound, Leezie gave another of her shrieking bursts of laughter. Grimly Robert set himself to endure the sound. He had bought time, he reminded himself, time to think, time to muster the powers of reason to his aid; and so the last laugh was yet to come.

The bell of Colstoun Parish Church began tolling at half-past eight o'clock on the evening of Robert Armett's tryst with the witch's daughter. Black Sarah and Leezie heard its note carrying faint but perfectly clear through the still evening air, and Leezie wondered aloud at the cause of its tolling.

'A funeral, of course,' Black Sarah told her, but absently, for her mind was too full of her triumph over the Armett family to permit of concern with other matters. Setting off to the churchyard with Leezie, she asked gleefully:

'Did you see young Armett's face when he came with the linen?'

Leezie laughed. 'I saw it!' She began to skip, scuffing her

bare toes in the summer dust, and boasting, 'I shall wear leather shoon when I am married to the Laird's son!'

'Aye, my lovely,' Black Sarah smiled fondly on her. 'And be Lady Colstoun too, some day, when the old Laird dies!'

Leezie laughed again and began moving along with an affectation of grandness; but her play-acting stopped as they turned into the lane running alongside the churchyard, for now the bell had stopped its tolling, and the funeral it had signalled was advancing slowly from the other end of the lane.

There was something oddly ominous in its appearance, too, although it was only a tiny cortège of four men bearing a coffin on their shoulders and two mourners following on foot. The men were cloaked in deepest black. Their faces were hidden by the bands of crêpe falling from their hats; and as they moved, tall and shadowless through the pale light of the summer's evening, it was only the steady shuffling of their feet that proclaimed them as men rather than dark spectres from some other world.

The witch and her daughter had halted at their appearance, and now they stayed motionless and half hidden by the hedge bordering the lane, while the men bore the coffin through the churchyard gate. The two mourners came into full view then—a young woman and an older one, both veiled and dressed in black—and with a gasp of astonishment, Leezie exclaimed:

'The Colstoun women—look! 'Tis Lady Colstoun and her daughter following the coffin!'

'Then who—' Black Sarah checked her own exclamation to stare more closely at the two mourners, then turned to nod at Leezie. It was true, her nod said. Even though her face was hidden by the veil, there was no mistaking the plump form of Lady Colstoun under those widow's weeds! And the gleam of long yellow hair under the veiling worn by the girl at her side undoubtedly belonged to Robert Armett's younger sister, Jenny.

'It must be the Laird's funeral, Leezie!' With excitement mounting in her voice, she followed the two women's progress through the churchyard gate. 'Aye, that's it! It must be the Laird. He was a gey sick man before I lifted the spell off him, after all, and now there is an end to him.'

'Then I shall be the new Lady Colstoun all the sooner!' Leezie grinned at her mother, glittering-eyed with delight.

Black Sarah nodded, and patted the pocket of her gown where the piece of Robert's body-linen lay stinking with the essences she had worked into it. 'You will, lovey, you will,' she agreed, and began to draw Leezie after her into the churchyard.

'Although I wish,' she added gloatingly, 'that the old man could have lived to see the work this charm will perform!'

She glanced up at the clock in the church tower, with its hands standing at five minutes to nine o'clock, and was tempted by a sudden idea. 'Wait here, lass,' she told Leezie. 'There is time yet for me to have a wee look at their weeping inside the church and join you again before young Armett arrives.'

'No—I am not wanting to stay alone!' Leezie made a panic grab for her mother's arm, and impatiently Black Sarah shook her off.

'But it's daylight yet, girl!'

Leezie glanced about her, shivering. 'No, it is not. This light has no shadows. 'Tis ghost-light—the day's ghost.'

Black Sarah stood undecided for a moment, but the prospect of witnessing the Armett family's grief was too near and to tempting to be missed.

'You will be quiet, then?' she demanded.

'As quiet as the dead old Laird,' Leezie promised, and laying hold of her mother again, crept silently with her through the open front door of the church.

There was a small vestibule beyond this door, with an inner door at the far side of it giving on to the main body of the church. Black Sarah led the way towards this inner door, and as she did so, there was a movement in the shadows behind the front door. A man stepped out from his hiding-place there—a tall stoop-shouldered man holding a key in his hand.

One long step took him across the vestibule, swinging the front door of the church closed as he moved. Black Sarah and Leezie spun to face the sound of its closing, and Leezie gave a little shriek of dismay as she saw the man turning the key in its lock. He faced about, holding the key in his hand again, and with a quick flush of rage, Black Sarah saw who had trapped her.

'Lawyer Bennet!' In a furious whisper, she spat out the name.

The tall man showed long yellow teeth in a caricature of a smile. 'I see you remember me from our last meeting in court, mistress, when I represented the Laird against you. But. . . .'

'But this is not a court of law!' Viciously Black Sarah interrupted him. 'And I know nothing of the Laird's death.'

'Who said you did?' Mr Bennet enquired mildly. 'But you have come to attend the funeral, all the same—just as my clients thought you would wish to do. And so now, if you please. . . .'

Politely he began ushering the two women into the church, and for all that rage was still nearly choking her, Black Sarah obeyed his urging hand. She had no choice but to do so, she admitted sullenly to herself, for the Armetts had been a great deal more cunning than she would have credited.

They had guessed she would be in the churchyard at nine o'clock to see her spell working, and purposely arranged the funeral for that time—guessing, too, that she would not be able to resist stealing into the church to gloat over it. So they had planned to trap her like this—hoping maybe to startle her into some admission of guilt over the Laird's death—and even to protest against their trap now would be taken as a sign of a guilty conscience.

But for all they had won this first round, Black Sarah vowed, she would still prove a match for them. They would get nothing out of her for their pains! With a sharp word and a single cruel pressure of her fingers, she quelled the small show of resistance Leezie was offering to Mr Bennet as he urged them down the central aisle between the pews of the church.

The mourners, she could see now, were seated in the front pews on either side of the aisle. She peered forward, trying to identify individuals among them, but the interior of the church was very dim and it was as much as she could do to distinguish the two Armett women among the row of bowed backs presented to her.

The Reverend Mr Campbell, the parish minister, stood at

the foot of the aisle dressed in hood and gown, his solemn face pale and very stern. Before him stood the trestle on which the coffin-bearers had laid their burden. The lid of the coffin was open, and the blur of white which was the shrouded corpse could be seen vaguely within it.

'Come forward.' Mr Campbell spoke softly but commandingly as Black Sarah hesitated at her first glimpse of this white blur. 'Come forward, woman, and view your work.'

Black Sarah stopped dead in her tracks. Mr Bennet stopped beside her. Leezie grasped the end of a pew and hung on with a determination that showed she had no intention of moving another step. This was the moment when she had to brave it out, Black Sarah decided, and boldly she called in reply:

'You have trapped me here, but all to no purpose, for the Laird's death is none of my work!'

'Who spoke of the Laird's death?'

The Laird of Colstoun rose from among the black-clad figures in the front pew, and turned to throw the challenge at her.

'Do as the minister says,' Mr Bennet ordered over her gasp of astonishment. 'Forward to look upon your work!'

He urged her on, and feeling the wiry strength behind the grip of his long, thin hand, she stumbled unresisting to the foot of the coffin. The black figures of the mourners rose to crowd about her, hemming her in against the coffin; and with a quick, indrawn break of shock, she recognized the waxy-white face of the shrouded corpse as that of Robert Armett. Lady Colstoun's voice came urgently then from among the mourners.

'Make her touch him! Lay her hand on the corpse!'

Hands grasped her own hands, forcing them towards the corpse; but with the instinct of self-preservation breaking sharply again through the confusion in her mind, she wrestled madly against this compulsion. A voice—the Laird's voice—panted in her ear:

'Come, Sarah, you know that one whose death was caused by a witch will bleed again if the witch touches him. But if you are innocent. . . .!'

'That is not law! It is not law—'tis only a saying!' Black

Sarah shrieked the words as her hands were forced down to rest on the corpse. In the same instant, Jenny Armett snatched the charmed linen out of the pocket of the witch's gown; and from beneath the hands crossed on the chest of the corpse, a red stain began spreading slowly over the whiteness of its shroud.

'Now deny it! Now deny you caused my son's death!' Black Sarah raised her stupefied gaze to see Lady Colstoun hissing furiously at her from the side of the coffin.

'I did not! I did not! I did not kill him!' The denials came babbling from her as she tried to pull her hands away. But Lady Colstoun was leaning over to uncross the arms of the corpse and show the bleeding knife-wound in its chest—a chest that showed naked through a ragged gap in the shroud. With one swift movement then, Jenny Armett placed the rag of charmed linen over this gap, and Lady Colstoun cried:

'It fits, you see! For that was the garment he wore next his heart at midnight on Midsummer's Eve—the garment he chose to wear rather than marry your daughter. And you killed him, for you forced that choice on him!'

'He died by his own hand—not mine!' Black Sarah jerked herself free at last, and backed away shrilling her protest. The mourners let her go, but there was someone else in her way now—Leezie; a wild-eyed, frantic Leezie, pushing one person after another aside to reach the coffin. Black Sarah grabbed her, but Leezie wrenched away and stood staring at the corpse. A whisper came from her, the whisper of Robert's name. The church clock boomed the first stroke of nine o'clock, and at this reminder of her broken schemes, Leezie shrieked the name aloud:

'*Robert!*'

The eyes of the corpse opened. Its head moved. Lady Colstoun exclaimed breathlessly. Jenny gasped, and the sound was echoed by Leezie and Black Sarah. With a low 'God help us!' Mr Campbell sank his face into his clasped hands.

Slowly, very slowly then, the corpse began to sit up in the coffin. Leezie screamed, and screamed again, backing away with her hands to her face and her eyes glaring with terror. The corpse began reaching out its shrouded arms to her, and she spun round on Black Sarah with her screaming shaping itself into words.

'You have enchanted a corpse to seek my love! You cast your spell on a dead man!'

Like a mad thing then, she pounced on Black Sarah, half-clinging in terror, half-attacking with rage; and screaming also. Black Sarah defended herself.

'But I never meant it, I never meant to bring him to you this way, Leezie! I did not *know* it was a piece of his shroud he brought me! I did not know he was dead when I cast the spell on it!'

A voice rang out above their continued screaming at one another, causing them both to fall suddenly silent and whirl round in its direction.

'There you have it! You have got what you always wanted, sir—Black Sarah's own admission of witchcraft, before witnesses!'

Robert Armett was sitting bolt upright in the coffin, a broad grin cracking the waxy-white paste of cosmetic that had made a death mask of his face. The shroud had fallen back from his shoulders. His father, the Laird, stood beside him, smiling also; and with her long yellow hair uncovered now, his sister Jenny was busily using her handkerchief to rub out the mark of the 'knife-wound' painted on his chest.

Black Sarah said stupidly: 'You—you are not dead! Then all this—the shroud, the pretended wound——' Speech failed her as she pointed a quivering hand at him.

'Represents the triumph of reason over superstition,' Robert finished for her, and grinned again as he squeezed another drop of 'blood' from the sponge soaked in red cochineal dye he had held secreted between the hands crossed on his chest. 'My reason, you see, Sarah; your superstition. It was only a trick to put you into a state of confusion and frighten Leezie—thus forcing you both to blurt out the truth without realizing you had done so!'

Leezie gave an inarticulate wailing sound, then darted forward with her hands clawing for his face, but was stopped short by two of the men who had carried the coffin. Black Sarah swung to face the Laird, but unperturbed by the hatred glaring from her eyes, he laid a benign hand on her shoulder and remarked:

'So I have all the evidence I need now, Sarah, for everyone here heard your confession.'

Black Sarah struck his hand away, mouthing in helpless rage at him. He shrugged. 'Take them away,' he instructed the coffin-bearers, and they began hustling Black Sarah and Leezie out of the church. Their progress down the aisle was a noisy resisting one, and it was not until the sound of it had died away that Lady Colstoun said thoughtfully:

'Well, husband, we have much to thank Robert for. You always said Black Sarah would never be convicted except on her own confession. And it was in the very moment she destroyed the image that you came back to health again.'

'I am sensible of all that, wife,' the Laird answered gravely. 'Most sensible.'

There was a general murmur of approval at this, then with creaky gallantry, Mr Bennet observed: 'But Master Robert's plan could not have succeeded, if I may say so, madam, without your most excellent play-acting over his supposed suicide.'

Lady Colstoun blushed. 'Jenny deserves congratulations too,' she pointed out. 'For where would we have been without her cosmetic help in creating the "corpse"?'

'All the same,' the Reverend Mr Campbell remarked uneasily, 'there was a serious lie at the heart of this charade, for Master Armett did *not* wear that shroud next his heart on Midsummer's Eve. We must pray God's mercy for that lie.'

Robert climbed stiffly from the coffin. 'A cloak, then, for pity's sake. It has been cold work playing the part of a dead man.'

Smilingly, the Laird loaned his cloak. In a stern voice, Mr Campbell said, 'Let us pray,' and under cover of the shuffling that ensued, Jenny Armett whispered to her brother:

'What do you suppose would have happened, Robert, if you really had worn that shroud next your heart at midnight on Midsummer's Eve?'

Robert felt an impulse to chuckle, but the impulse died as

he remembered the evil force of Black Sarah's personality, and the uncanny influence she had exerted on him.

'To tell you the truth, Jenny,' he said with a little shiver, 'I am not sure what would have happened. But I think—I think that maybe some day my ghost might have been forced to tryst with Leezie.'

Then he bowed his head, thinking of an evening world of light that was not daylight; a shadowless, still and dreaming world where a witch's daughter might have wandered seeking a lost tryst, and an enchanted ghost-lover might have come gliding at last to her.

When I was a child we used to listen with growing impatience for the music of the first cuckoo. While we waited we chanted, 'In April come he will. In May sing all day. In June change his tune. In July away he fly. In August go he must.'

In those long-ago days when I was a child that was exactly how cuckoos behaved. Some time in April we heard the first call. In May they never stopped singing their lovely signature tune. In June the tune changed. Then in July very few cuckoos were heard and myself I never heard one at all in August. All cuckoos had disappeared.

If, as I did, you lived in Sussex then you were particularly cuckoo conscious, for a place called Hailsham had the undisputed right to hear the first cuckoo. Its voice was first heard at a fair called Heffle Fair where, as everybody knew, an old woman let the first cuckoo out of her basket. So well known was this fact that if someone wrote to a newspaper to say they heard the first cuckoo and the date was before Heffle Fair, the editor would write back to say he was afraid they had made a mistake for the old woman had not yet opened her basket.

Nowadays cuckoos are not what they were. This year, though I listened all over the country, I never heard a cuckoo at all—not even one.

But Helen Cresswell, who wrote this story, let her Martin hear the cuckoo's song many times, and as well brought the country alive with wild flowers. So alive that every scent and colour that spells summer is blazingly alive as you read.

This is the last story in this book so it pleases me that a piece of real summer is yours to keep, and yours perhaps to take out and re-read on a cold, drizzly November day.

HELEN CRESSWELL

The Cuckoo

Martin was surprised to find that he liked the country, after all. It was hardly at all as he had imagined it would be. He had had a vague idea that it would be all ducks and geese and noise, wielding pitchforks, tractors, milking cows. Instead, it was very quiet. It had none of the suburban peace of long, tree-lined avenues and shady gardens that Martin was used to. It had, once away from his uncle's farm and the scattered cottages, a slow, breathing peace of its own that was at once exciting and a little frightening. Gingerly, half afraid of spoiling something, he made his advances.

'You get out into the fresh air all you can,' Aunt Anne told him. 'White as a ghost you look. We can't send you back looking like that.'

First red, then white, Martin thought. The scarlet of the fever had faded though once it had seemed as if it never would, in those hours and days—or was it weeks?—of aching and tossing and endless burning. He looked a little enviously at his cousin Bob, who was thirteen, a year older than himself, and brown skinned, tough enough to take on a boy of fifteen with his fists and beat him, as he had done only last week. When Martin had arrived Bob had shown him the fading scars and bruises, casually, but seeming to vaunt his own strength at the side of Martin's pallor and weakness.

Now, after only a day or two, the envy was only lukewarm, diluted by the discovery that Bob was near the bottom of his class at the local school, that he didn't learn French and never read books. Besides, Bob was at school every day and they only met in the evening, so there had been no time for really taking each other's measure. Despite this Martin felt, oddly, that they already knew each other as well as they ever would.

On the third day of his visit Martin set out straight after breakfast to explore in a new direction. In the distance, from his bedroom window, he could see a hill crowned by a small wood or spinney.

'Got your flower book?' Aunt Anne asked him. Martin shook his head and hurried away: he had, though—concealed in the inside pocket of his jacket. He had one about birds, too. It had been his mother's idea.

'You'll be able to identify all the flowers and birds you come across,' she told him. 'There'll be lots at this time of year. It'll make your walks more interesting.'

His explorations yesterday had been interrupted every few minutes by references to his books. It seemed as if there was not a bird or flower that he knew. He began to look at daisies and buttercups with positive affection, grateful for their familiarity. Back at the farmhouse he had laid a selection of flowers out on the kitchen table.

'That's hawksbeard,' he had told them. 'And this is broom.'

'Hawksbit,' Bob had said. 'And gorse.'

Martin felt himself redden.

'It's in my book,' he said defensively. 'That can't be wrong.'

'Look,' Bob said. 'I've known them since I was a kid, book or no book. That's hawkbit and the other's gorse. Right, Mum?'

'Right,' she said. 'Though I can see how you could confuse them. You'll soon learn to tell the difference, Martin.'

Later, in his room, he had checked them again. The yellow flower had sharp green spines, instead of leaves. It *was* gorse. He checked the leaves of the other plant, too. Bob had been right.

It was late May and hot already, but looking about him he had for a moment the illusion that the fields and hedges were still scattered with patches of unmelted snow. Hawthorn and cow parsley spread great white splashes over the rich green. But Martin did not know their names. Dutifully he stopped and took out his book. A few minutes' thumbing and searching and he had identified them.

'Cow parsley,' he repeated.

He looked again at the great drifts of white. Knowing their names did not seem to have brought him any nearer to them. It suddenly seemed to him that the book in his hand put a gulf between them. The hot May landscape was transformed into a stranger—hostile, even.

'What does it matter?' he muttered. 'What does it *matter* what their names are?'

Then he heard the cuckoo. Its notes came clearly over the still roads from the wood on the hill, and in that moment the day was suddenly like any other May day that Martin had ever known. He had heard that song a thousand times before, mocking his searches over neighbouring gardens, charting invisible flights across the quiet avenues.

Instinctively he started towards the wood at a half run, making for the familiar voice. He toiled up the hillside, keeping to the narrow lane because he was not yet used to open fields and tracklessness. With the instinct of a town-dweller he followed paths already made for him.

As he neared the wood the cuckoo's voice grew louder yet none-the-less mysterious, beckoning from the muffled green shade. He plunged from the heat and sunlight of the meadow into the instant chill and shadow under the trees. The sky was lost now and he ran through whirling slats of sun and shadow, ducking and diving under low branches while the cuckoo went over him time and again—or else the echo did.

When he stopped he was at the heart of the little wood. Panting, he heard the cuckoo cross again, its voice louder now than he had ever heard it. Though he strained his eyes into the layered boughs and knew maddeningly that the bird was not a stone's throw off, there was not a sign of it. Then, as if suddenly tired of the game, the cuckoo made off, the notes grew rapidly fainter. Martin was left standing there, alone in the all at once quiet wood.

There seemed nothing left to do. He began to retrace his steps, making roughly in the direction he had come from, though there was no real track. Eventually he came upon a worn path, and followed that, knowing that it must sooner or later take him to the edge of the wood. Soon light appeared between the trees and he found himself standing at the top of a field, and far round to the right he could see the road up the hill from the village. He

stood hesitating, uncertain where to go, because there was a long morning still in front of him, and he had nothing really to do. Then he saw the old man and the hut.

It was on the very edge of the wood to his left, in a kind of bay or inlet, where the field curved into the trees. It seemed to be a rough shelter, rather than a hut, made of branches and twigs, with a tarpaulin thrown over. The man was seated on an up-turned wooden crate, hunched over as if he were making something with his hands. As Martin watched he got up, and in doing so, turned and met his gaze.

'Good morning,' Martin said. Was it a gamekeeper? Was he himself trespassing?

'Mornin'.' The old man's bearded face was placid and unsurprised. He didn't look like a man who had just caught someone trespassing. His eyes moved beyond Martin and rested on something there, and he said quietly,

'Don't ee move, now. Just act very quiet and nateral then turn, very slow, and look up there in that birch, see.'

Wondering, Martin did as he was bid.

'See un?'

'A squirrel!' cried Martin. He clapped his hand to his mouth too late and saw only a brief flash of reddish brown and a settling of disturbed leaves, and it was gone.

'I'm sorry!'

'Oh, don't ee fret. He'll be back. He come right here, sometime. He'll walk across your feet if you've something for him. He'll be back.'

He lifted an iron pot and carried it over to the other side of the shelter where a small fire was smoking.

'He lives here!' thought Martin. With his rough clothes and beard he might easily be a tramp. Except that he didn't act like a tramp. There was something calm and settled about him. Martin advanced.

'Do you live here?' he asked.

The man turned and looked at him.

'You're not up from the village, then? No, no. You won't be from there.'

'I'm staying down at Wolds Farm,' Martin told him. 'I've never been here before.'

'No. No. . . .' He seemed to have forgotten the question Martin had asked him.

'What's that you've got, then?' he asked. 'Making shooters, are ye?'

Surprised Martin looked down and realized that he meant the bunch of cow parsley that he was still clutching.

'It's cow parsley,' he said casually.

'Oh it's that, all right,' agreed the old man. 'A bit juicy yet, though, for hollowing. Another month or so'll see it right.'

Now Martin came right into the encampment.

'What do you mean?' he asked.

'You ain't never made a shooter out of one of them?'

Martin shook his head.

'When they're oldish and the sap's dried out, they're hollered out nateral, almost. Many's the shooter I've had from them when I was a lad. Pipes to play out of 'em there is, too, if you've a mind to it.'

Martin examined the stem of the plant where he had broken it off. Sure enough, the stem was wide and hollow, though still green and moist. This was not one of the biggest he'd seen, by a long way. On the way home he would find a really big one, maybe even one that was already hardening and 'drying out'.

The old man had finished with his cooking and was sitting again, whittling.

'Do you live here?' asked Martin again.

'I do,' he returned, 'and then I don't. Most summers I comes up. I've an old place of my own, t'other side village. I like it up here, summers. More company, like.'

Martin, following his gaze to the hot meadows beyond and the slowly wading cows, thought the remark a strange one.

'With all the birds, I suppose you mean?' he asked at last. 'And the animals—like the squirrel?'

'Aye. That's it.'

He went on whittling. He seemed quite content with silence. Martin felt that if he himself did not speak, nor would he. They could sit there all morning, the two of them, without a word between them. He sat down himself and watched the old man's fingers. At the first the silence oppressed him. People *always* talked when there were two or more of them. Perhaps he had offended the man? A glance at the quiet, intent face told him that this was not the explanation. He seemed to have forgotten that Martin was there at all.

Oddly, the longer the silence went on, the more companionable it became. Martin began to feel himself at ease. He stopped wondering what he ought to say. He was aware of the song of a particular bird nearby, singled out from the rest. He began to notice a pattern in it, a subtle but unmistakeable repetition. At the same time, another part of him was noticing the lazy, rhythmical lumbering of the cattle as they went knee deep in a deluge of buttercups. In the distance he watched another herd. They moved slow and stately like chess pieces against the side of the hill.

He had no idea how long they sat there, but all at once he felt that it was time to go. He stood up. The old man lifted his head.

'I'll be going along now, then,' said Martin.

'Aye,' agreed the other. He seemed not the least curious.

'May I come again?' asked Martin. 'Tomorrow?'

He nodded. Martin went to the edge of the clearing, then looked back.

'My name's Martin,' he said. He could not go without giving the meeting some kind of realness, solidity. 'What's yours?'

As he spoke he had a sudden wild feeling that perhaps the old man *hadn't* a name, that he was just the Old Man, with capital letters, like a character in a book or play.

'Tom. They all call me that. Tom.'

'Goodbye, Tom.' Martin turned and hurried away, deliberately crashing and trampling because really he did not want to go.

He went back the next day, and the next. On the third day, Tom was repairing the roof to his shelter, and showed Martin how it was done, dexterously weaving the branches Martin had helped him to collect.

'Like a bird making a nest, really.'

'Aye,' agreed Tom. 'Though not so clever.'

He showed Martin how to select branches suitable for the work, testing them for springiness, rejecting any that cracked or split when they were bent into a loop.

'But don't throw 'em away,' he warned. 'Them's for the fire, the snappers. Aught that snaps'll likely burn.'

Tom did not talk very much. Martin became used to this early in their friendship. His rare remarks were always to do with the task in hand, or something he had just noticed. If Martin asked him a question, about a bird or a flower or tree, he would answer, and then silence would fall again. There was never really any conversation, such as Martin was used to with his father, or friends' fathers, or teachers at school. He recognized Tom's oddity, and for the most part respected it. It's because he's always lived in the country, he thought. It's true, really. They *are* a bit slow. Another peculiarity of Tom's was that he didn't seem afraid of doing nothing at all. For minutes on end he would sit motionless, his eyes gazing into the distance, and yet missing nothing as Martin learned to realize.

For some reason that he did not trouble to explain to himself Martin did not mention his visits to Tom to the others. It might have been simply for the sheer excitement of keeping a secret. Or it might have been that he felt he was making his first, tentative footholds on the country around him, that he was beginning to make it his own, in his own way. Some inner sense warned him that his uncle, aunt and cousin, country bred and careless, would misunderstand.

'You're getting out a lot,' Aunt Anne would say, pleased. 'Not that I know what you find to do all day out there by yourself. But I suppose boys will always find something. It's good colour you're getting, anyhow. Your mother'll be pleased.'

On the Saturday of his second week Martin went up to the spinney as usual. He found Tom rummaging in his storehouse.

'I s'll have to get down to the village,' he said. 'Food's low.'

Martin already knew that Tom went very early to a nearby farm for his bread, milk and butter.

'Can I come with you?' he asked. 'I could help carry.'

Tom hesitated.

'You—if I was to tell you, and you was to write it—what if *you* could bring 'em for me?'

For once the old man was unlike his usually calm self. He seemed troubled.

'I never use shops much, d'ye see,' he explained. 'All my things come to the door, home, see?'

'But you must *sometimes* go down to the village while you're up here,' said Martin.

'Oh aye, aye, I do,' agreed Tom. Still his face was worried and anxious looking.

'I'll go,' said Martin. He found a pencil and paper. 'You just tell me what you want, and I'll write them down.'

'Ah!' Tom's face lightened. 'That's good lad. Thank ye, my lad, thank ye.'

Martin made the list. It was a long one. Then Tom fetched an old raffia shopping bag and a carrier from his hut and two pound notes. Martin set off for the village.

At the main store, Mrs Moffet was curious and talkative. Her eyes flicked rapidly over him, taking in the shabby bag and soiled carrier. Martin handed her the list.

'We haven't been seeing much of you while you've been here,' she said. 'Good time you're having?'

'Yes, thank you.'

'Going home tomorrow, I hear.'

'Yes.'

'Your aunt was in yesterday with the order. A lot of things she's left off, my word.'

Martin was silent.

'Would you like to leave the list, and me just send these things up to the house with the rest?'

'No!' cried Martin. 'No, thank you. I'll take them.'

She began to collect the items, whipping them down from the shelves and pencilling their prices on the list.

'There we are.' She ran the pencil expertly down the list. 'One pound thirteen and four. Going to pay, are you?'

Martin handed her the money.

'Give me your bag, dearie, and I'll pack them in. Quite a lot to carry, for you. Oh! My goodness! I could have sworn——!'

'What?'

'This bag. I could have sworn it was that one of poor old Tom Payne's. It—I *declare* it is. Well I never. Not poorly, is he?'

'No, thank you,' said Martin. 'He's very well. I just offered to get these things for him.'

He did not miss her sharp glance.

'Oh, I see. Up in the spinney, is he? We've not seen him yet this year.'

'Yes he is.'

'Mmmm. Well, there you are. Now, take care.' She lowered her voice. 'He's harmless enough, we all know that. But take care, and don't hang about.'

Martin, baffled, stared at her. She was leaning forward over the counter, her eyes intense behind her spectacles. Was she a little mad?

'Yes, well, thank you,' he said, and picked up the bags. 'Goodbye.'

He set off back for the spinney. The climb this morning seemed twice as far and as steep as usual, despite the fact that he now by-passed the roads and followed a track through the fields that Tom had shown him. As he reached the stile into the last field, he heard the cuckoo, calling loudly from the trees above him, mocking, as it had done on that first day.

He put the bags down and looked about him, wiping his arm across his wet forehead. The song ran out over the hot, dry fields, it seemed to be all round him, like echoes in a cave. He plodded on up the slope, the bags dragging low, brushing the grasses, and all the while the cuckoo's call seemed right above him. He had heard it every single day during the last fortnight, making its secret circles round the wood, but as he reached the edge of the clearing its voice was so loud that he could hardly believe that the bird was not right overhead. He dropped the bags again and looked up.

There, at last, the cuckoo went, right along the edge of the wood, calling in flight, a big brown bird flying in the open, a plain brown bird, a dead legend.

Then it was gone. The cries grew fainter. Tom sat with his head turned in the direction the bird had gone.

'Saw her, this time, did ye?' he said. 'Told you. No magic to a cuckoo. She's there to see, if you're there to look.'

'Yes.' Martin was filled with a curious sense of betrayal. Cuckoos should be heard and not seen.

'I'm going home tomorrow,' he heard himself say. 'I'm glad.'

'Aye. Ye got the things, did ye?'

Tom began to store his groceries in the lean-to hut that served as a larder. Martin had thrown himself down on the ground, uncomfortably hot and filled with a sudden and surprising home-sickness. With the flight of the cuckoo in full view, a spell had been broken. For the first time he found himself looking at Tom critically, and thought, 'He's pretty grubby, really. Shouldn't think he washes much. Mum'd have a fit.' He visualized his parents' car driving into the farmyard next day, his father, mother, the journey home, and his own room and things again. He remembered the scale model of a train he'd been making, left half finished.

'Ye'll not be coming up again, then?' Tom had finished stowing his provisions now and was standing in front of the hut, facing him.

'I don't suppose so,' said Martin. Now that the time had come he did not know how to say goodbye, because in a sense he did not really know Tom at all. He had sat up here for hours with him, learned from him and listened to him, and for all that he was still a stranger. Tom was fishing in his pocket and now he held out his hand.

'Here,' he said, 'I thought mebbe you'd like it.'

Martin went forward and took it, a wooden pipe, beautifully carved. He lifted it to his lips and blew and the notes were sweet and liquid.

'Thank you!' he cried, 'It's marvellous! Just what I wanted!'

'Sings true,' nodded the old man, and seated himself again in his usual place, gazing for a few minutes out from the shadow of the wood to the sun-washed meadows, almost lost again.

'I'd better be going then,' Martin said.

'Aye.'

'Perhaps I'll see you again. Next year, perhaps.'

'Mebbe.'

'Well, goodbye, then. And thanks for everything—especially the pipe.'

Tom nodded and Martin turned and went. As he went out from beneath the shadow of the wood and into the heat and brightness of the meadow, he turned and waved. He saw an arm raised in answering salute, and then he ran, suddenly wanting the parting to be over.

In the farmhouse he found Bob already back from his Saturday morning jobs about the farm.

'Me'n the lads are going over by Stepping this afternoon,' he told Martin casually. 'Wakes are on. Coming?'

'All right,' Martin heard himself say. As soon as he had said it he was surprised, sorry even. Bob's friends were big, noisy village lads and so far he'd avoided them. He avoided all gangs, if it came to that, even at home.

In his room he took out the carved pipe and looked at it again. It was beautiful. It must have taken hours of Tom's steady, patient carving.

'I wish I'd given him something,' he thought. His eyes swept over his belongings, littered about the room, half packed ready for the next day. His eyes fell upon the two books his mother had given him. 'He's one person who doesn't need those,' he thought. Then he saw his torch, a powerful one with a two hundred foot beam that he'd bought last winter. '*That*'d be useful,' he decided.

Stepping was a village that lay on the other side of the spinney. He could set out with Bob and the rest, then say he'd changed his mind, and branch off on his own. They'd think it was queer, but let them.

It seemed odd to set off up the now familiar road towards

the spinney in a gang. He had travelled it so many times alone and knew it so well that he felt the others to be intruders—and noisy ones, at that. They shouted and laughed and cut switches from the hedges, making incomprehensible remarks, remote as foreigners. When they reached the gate where he had intended to leave them, the leader vaulted carelessly over it and set off up the field over the very route he always took himself.

'Where are we going?' he asked Bob, who was loitering in the rear with one or two cronies, 'I thought you said they were going to Stepping?'

'We are.' Bob spat out the grass he was chewing. 'Quickest way, up over the top. Brings us right down by the bridge.'

Martin hesitated, ready to turn back. But he felt the hard shape of the torch in his pocket, and kept on after them. He could lose them in the spinney—slip off on his own. *That* lot would never notice. He trailed after them, his eyes fixed on the turf, already as miserable as he had known he would be.

What happened next happened with the suddenness and clarity of nightmare. He heard Bob's voice——

'Look! It's loony Tom—the wild man of the woods!'

He heard too the cuckoo, right overhead, and looking up he saw that the gang had veered across the fields and were within fifty yards of the clearing where Tom's hut stood. As the cuckoo shouted again and again he saw Tom, who had been sitting in his usual place, stand and stare down towards the approaching boys.

'Good old Tom!' shouted a voice. 'It's the old cuckoo himself. Hark at him! Cuckoo! Cuckoo!'

'Cuckoo! Cuckoo! Cuckoo!' the rest took up the rowdy mocking chorus, drowning the bird's calls, drowning everything.

'Come on, Cuckoo, let's hear you sing!'

'The Cuckoo's built a nest!'

Martin clutched at Bob's sleeve.

'Stop it! Stop it!' he cried. The sleeve was jerked away. Just then Tom looked, straight at him it seemed, and without a word turned and went away across the clearing and into his hut.

The chorus followed him.

'Cuckoo! Cuckoo!'

Martin turned and began to run headlong, jarring over the uneven turf, and he felt the torch leap from his pocket as he went, and still he ran, leaving it to lie there. He swung himself over the gate and ran on down the lane until at last he was forced to stop.

Beyond the noisy gulping of his own breathing there was only the heat and the stillness. He forced himself to look back, up towards the spinney. No one was in sight. They were in the spinney now, joke over, crashing their way towards the joyrides of Stepping wakes. Faint and far away he heard the cuckoo calling.

'Thank *goodness* I'm going home,' he heard himself say under his breath. 'Thank *goodness*.'

He dragged his eyes away from the glare of buttercups and headed for home. The cuckoo had meant summer, his whole life long. Even here it had greeted him, a familiar voice in a hostile landscape. And now he never wanted to hear it again. Never.

I shall finish the book with a poem. What I wanted was a real bumble bee-ox-eyed daisy soft-lapping waves of a poem. Something which, whenever you read it, brought summer into your heart. The trouble was I wanted a modern poem and I do not think modern poets often write that sort of poetry. Then I remembered Shepherd and Shepherdess—*really good modern pastoral poetry. If you do not already know it I hand it to you as a little present.*

Shepherd and Shepherdess

O for our upland meads,
Wherein of childhood's deeds
To prattle, fancy leads
Past rills, and groves of trees.

For camomile and orchis,
Fritillary, our search is,
A wreath that lovers purchase
With a sweet kiss in the eyes.

By shade of ash and laurels
We will forget our quarrels,
Sourer than August sorrels
Nibbled with bread and cheese.

Kerchiefed tomatoes red
Here on a hillock spread:
Fetch water from the stream,
That fancy here may dream.

Pleasures so kind as these
The silly minutes please,
Our flocks upon the leas
May scatter far as wandering bees.

Thomas Hennell

Contents

The compiler and publishers are grateful to the following for permission to include copyright material:

Curtis Brown Ltd., for 'The Outlaws' by Ursula Moray Williams. © Ursula Moray Williams, 1973.
Elizabeth Carney for 'Teresa'. © Elizabeth Carney, 1973.
Curtis Brown Ltd., for the extract from *Gerald. A Portrait* by Daphne du Maurier.
J. M. Dent & Sons Ltd., for 'Andy' from *The Great Brain* by John D. Fitzgerald. Copyright © 1967 by John D. Fitzgerald.
Curtis Brown Ltd., for 'Lost Treasure' by Dorothy Clewes from *Girl Annual*.
Curtis Brown Ltd., for 'Loving and Giving' by Rumer Godden. © Rumer Godden, 1973.
Curtis Brown Ltd., on behalf of the Dunsany Estate, for 'The True Story of the Hare and the Tortoise' by Lord Dunsany.
Helen Hoke Associates Ltd., for 'The Trees' by Margaret Mahy. © Margaret Mahy, 1973.
James MacGibbon, executor of the late Stevie Smith, for 'The Heavenly City' by Stevie Smith.
Sarah Stafford Smith for 'The Moonlight Bird'. © Sarah Stafford Smith, 1973.
A. M. Heath & Co. Ltd., for 'The Midsummer Charm' by Mollie Hunter. © Mollie Hunter, 1973.
A. M. Heath & Co. Ltd., for 'The Cuckoo' by Helen Cresswell from 'The Cornhill'.

Every effort has been made to trace owners of copyright and, in at least one case, without success. It is hoped that any such omission will be pardoned.

STAY ON

Here are details of other exciting TARGET titles. If you cannot obtain these books from your local bookshop, or newsagent, write to the address below listing the titles you would like and enclosing cheque or postal order—*not* currency—including 7p per book to cover packing and postage; 2–4 books, 5p per copy; 5–8 books, 4p per copy.

TARGET BOOKS,
Universal-Tandem Publishing Co.,
14 Gloucester Road,
London SW7 4RD

THE CREEPY-CRAWLY BOOK 30p

Lucy Berman

0 426 10241 x

What living thing would you *least* like to be left alone with in a room late at night? A large, hairy, tropical spider? A poisonous snake? A large rat?—with red eyes, of course! Or would you go in for smaller fry like a mouse, or a scorpion, or an ant? Are these unpleasant creatures in every case as nasty as they seem? *Strictly for older boys and girls! Illustrated.*